MW00986599

Mrs. Blennerhassett on the Marietta Trail

To the fair Isle, reverts the pleasing dream,
  Again thou risest in thy green attire,
Fresh, as at first, thy blooming graces seem;
  Thy groves, thy fields, their wonted sweets respire.
Again thou'rt all my heart could e'er desire.
  O! why, dear Isle, art thou not still my own?
Thy charms could then for all my griefs atone.

—From the Deserted Isle

Blennerhassett Island from the West Virginia side heights, painting 1938

Blennerhassett Island
in Romance and Tragedy

The Authentic Story of Blennerhassett Island
with the Burr Episode entwined about it
The Romance and Mystery of the Blennerhassetts
Burr under Footlights and Shadows
Tragedy of Theodosia Burr

By Minnie Kendall Lowther

Author of

*Mount Vernon, Its Children, Its Romances, Its Allied Families
and Mansions
Friendship Hill, and other works*

*One of the most colorful chapters
in American History*

A Study
From Authentic and Indisputable Sources

THE TUTTLE PUBLISHING COMPANY, Inc.
RUTLAND, VERMONT

Reprint issued in 1974
by Mrs. A. Karl (Eloise) Summers

Reprinted 1989 by
McClain Printing Company
Parsons, West Virginia
For TransAllegheny Books, Inc.
Parkersburg, West Virginia

Standard Book Number 87012-164-2

McCLAIN PRINTING COMPANY
PARSONS, WEST VIRGINIA 26287

PRINTED IN THE U. S. A.

This little volume is dedicated
to the new Blennerhassett that is
rising from its ruins in the spirit
of the truth and justice of the New Day

Authenticated Picture

Blennerhassett Mansion and Court

On having this book re-published, I wish to dedicate it to my aunt, the author, Minnie Kendall Lowther, who never lost faith in her belief that someday the Island would become a National Shrine.

Eloise Summers (Mrs. A. Karl)

Mrs. Blennerhassett   Harman Blennerhassett
Aaron Burr   Theodosia Burr Alston

The Author

Preface

It is our belief that Minnie Kendall Lowther was imbued with the spirit of prophesy when she wrote: "This little volume is dedicated to the new Blennerhassett that is rising from its ruins in the spirit of the truth and justice of the New Day."

In September, 1970, the Blennerhassett Island development project originated with Parkersburg's Sesquicentennial Celebration Committee, of which we were chairman and secretary, respectively. Since that time we have read everything we could lay hands on concerning Blennerhassett Island! This book is to us one of the most enjoyable and inspiring of the many publications we have read.

We especially like Miss Lowther's stated purpose in writing this volume as "an attempt at a sincere and impartial presentation of one of the most colorful chapters in American History. . . ." Not only were these chapters colorful—but the results of Burr's and Blennerhassett's dreams of empire had an important and lasting influence on the development of our nation. Dr. Edwin S. Corwin, Professor Emeritus of Jurisprudence at Princeton University, said of Burr's trial for treason at Richmond, Virginia, that it is regarded as "the greatest criminal trial in American history and one of the notable trials in the annals of law." The trial established the independence of the Supreme Court and the Doctrine of Executive (Presidential) Privilege, so current in today's news. As pointed out by Miss Lowther, Burr was not only acquitted of treason, but also of a misdemeanor charge, facts which his enemies tended to overlook. (Blennerhassett was never brought to trial.)

A musical drama concerning the segment of the lives of Harman and Margaret Blennerhassett when they were involved with Aaron Burr has been completed; West Virginia's Governor Moore has expressed the hope that this drama will be produced on Blennerhassett Island as part of our state's contribution to the nation's bicentennial in 1976.

The Blennerhassett Drama Association has been incorporated; the prime purpose of this non-profit corporation is to secure the building of an amphitheater for the production of the drama, *Eden on the River*, on the Island. The eight-county Little Kanawha Resource Conservation and Development Blennerhassett Committee has joined with the BDA in its efforts to realize its dream, as have many interested citizens on both sides of the Ohio River. In fact, we have received encouragement from many parts of the United States. A Legislative Commission, the Blennerhassett Historical Commission, has been very active, and in January, 1974, received $70,000 from the Joint Committee on Government and Finance for the development of a master plan for the Island. The E. I. Du Pont de Nemours Company, owners of Blennerhassett Island, has indicated to the Commission its willingness to cooperate in a manner beneficial to the interest of all concerned.

Thus to date it seems that a re-birth of Margaret's "Eden" may become a reality soon.

During the year 1973 feasibility studies were conducted in three phases: archaeological, the drama, and architectural. These studies proved unqualifiedly that Miss Lowther's dream and ours is indeed feasible. Manifold benefits will accrue to the entire area surrounding Blennerhassett Island from such a development as we envision.

Archaeological exploration carried out during the summer of 1973 disclosed the long-buried foundations of the mansion, giving us its accurate measurements for the first time; the main house was $54'x38'10''$, two porticos $13'2''$ wide and $37'$ long connected the end wings which measured $26'x26'$. Of interest nationwide was the discovery of a prehistoric palisaded village of the Fort Ancient Culture, the northernmost found to date. It is the archaeologists' belief that Blennerhassett Island has been occupied since approximately 12,000 B.C., and that there lies beneath its surface enough material of historic and pre-historic value to require thirty years to explore properly!

We salute Minnie Kendall Lowther, a woman of high courage and ideals! She was born in Fonzo, West Virginia, March 17, 1869, daughter of William G. and Emma Jane Kendall Lowther. While a young woman she was thrown from a horse, suffering a spinal injury that forced her to spend eighteen years in a wheelchair. Despite this restriction she taught elementary school in Ritchie County, West Virginia, and was editor of a Buckhannon, West Virginia, newspaper. A student of history, careful and tireless researcher, her days were spent in writing and studying until her death, September 18, 1947. She is buried in the family plot in Harrisville, West Virginia.

This book is being re-issued by the author's niece, Mrs. A. Karl Summers, of Parkersburg, West Virginia, in response to the great resurgence of interest in the Blennerhassett story.

Mr. and Mrs. A. Beauchamp Smith III
President and Secretary,
Blennerhassett Drama Association

January, 1974

Foreword

No two persons see an incident just alike; no two persons interpret it alike; and consequently for this reason, perhaps, more than from wilful misrepresentation, such medleys of contradictions confront the seeker for facts. Prejudices, too, play their part; catering to public whims and fancies add to the dilemma, but despite all this, the purpose of this little volume is an attempt at a sincere and impartial presentation of one of the most colorful chapters in American History. Its sources of information are first-hand diaries, journals, letters, which were penned in a confidence that never dreamed of publicity, court proceedings, etc., which sets aside much that has gone before.

Mystery enveloped Harman Blennerhassett. The charge of conspiracy and disloyalty to his country, so overshadowed the glory of Burr's early life, as to send him to his grave in old age branded as a traitor, though no such charge has ever been substantiated. This story removes the veil, discloses the mystery, and bespeaks tardy justice and fairness to all.

Like the average American, the Author shared these prejudices, which were instilled into her mind by history from her earliest recollection. Burr was to her the embodiment of all that was evil when she began this research, several years ago. At the time of her visit to the Island, he stood out in fancy right beside the old well, as an "engaging devil," impersonating the talking serpent of the fair Eden of old. But investigation removed her ignorance, arrested her prejudices, changed her mental picture. Aaron Burr now takes his place upon the canvas as a brilliant American, full of caprice, like all the rest of Adam's race, with just as many virtues as numerous other public men, who have gone down to their graves under blare of trumpet, and paeans of praise.

Burr was brilliant far beyond the average man of his or any other time; and for this grave (?) fault, jealousy demanded that he be removed from public life. Just or unjust he paid the penalty in the fullest measure. Few men in all history have called forth such acclaim; few have been subject to such denunciation; and none have ever been hurled from "such dizzy heights" into such an abyss of darkness and despair.

Blennerhassett, in his evident stupidity, aroused no such antagonism, but want of judgment, and the lack of good common, every-day sense was his undoing.

Among the more recent writers who have rallied to Burr's standard, we find none abler than Beveridge in his "Life of John Marshall"; Samuel H. Wandell and Meade Minnegrode, in their joint-two-volume, "Aaron Burr," 1925, which are among the printed authorities quoted in this book.

M. K. L.

Contents

BLENNERHASSETT MANSION 1800

Claimed to be a drawing from description given by Colonel Barker,
the architect, but we have been unable to authenticate it

List of Illustrations

The Old Sycamore, 1921

The Winecellar Tree, 1921

Part II

The Bungalow that marks the site of Mansion and Court to-day,
with the tree that grew out of the winecellar

1

Blennerhassett Island

The occupant of the small craft that drifted down the current a century and a third ago marveled over the beauty and magnificence of an Island within the embrace of the Ohio River, two miles below what is now Parkersburg, West Virginia. A veritable terrestrial paradise —such as might have suggested the magic of some Aladdin's Lamp, spread out before him, and called forth the puzzling question, "Why such a palace in the wilderness"?

The passenger on the more modern steamer that plowed the river for many years later, still beheld this island, so picturesquely endowed by Nature; but its enchanted castle was gone; its magnificence had vanished; and a spirit of desolation brooded over the place where beauty had once reigned so supreme. This was Blennerhassett Island, whose blended charm, romance, mystery, and adventure has held the attention of a world, since the dawn of the Nineteenth Century; and still gives no sign of abated interest.

It was in the flitting lights and shadows of a hot July day—1921, that we first stood upon it. The difficulty in reaching it was finally overcome by a boatman on the Ohio side, who agreed to row us over and come again at an appointed time; for the custom of shouting across the river was a bit too uncertain for our voice.

As we followed the winding pathway up from the landing, through woodland and briery opening, it required a vivid imagination to realize that such reputed culture and splendor could ever have existed here where not a semblance of it remained, save what was marked by ruins. Surely this could not be the Enchanted Isle of the fascinating stories of our childhood. But the sight of the old mansion seemed to bring the realization that this must be the "Deserted Isle" of the sequel to the story, at least. A fancied footfall of the once gracious mistress and the heavier tread of the ungainly master seemed to echo down the corridor of the years that lay between, as we gazed upon the ruins of the old brick passageway to the basement and winecellar of their day, which was just about all that remained of the once-famed mansion. A small bungalow marked the site of the court; and a stately sycamore, which had its roots in the winecellar, lifted its head protectingly over the iron inclosure, which enfolded the caps of the old gateway, and added shade and color to the somber scene. The old well, with its inimitable waters, though modernized by new curb and cement surroundings, still quenched the thirst of the visitor as it had in Blenner-hassett's time. The same old trees that fanned the brow of the "engaging Stranger" when he so blithely entered this Eden in the long ago, bent their shadowing branches to the breezes and invited one to linger in their friendly shade.

The Island had long been divided into various farms with individual tenants, and we caught an interesting glimpse of this farm-life and its crops on this mid-summer day; and partook of the hospitality of one of the tenants at the noon-day hour.

The old brick house, built in 1833, with its outstanding masonry in the cellar, was still occupied, and a pioneer woodpile, with axe upon it, lay but a few steps from the door. Not far distant stood the old sycamore, so noted as a hiding place in Indian times. Cottages for tenants, a barn, and other outbuildings just about completed the improvements of the place.

With our rambles and picture-taking at an end, we returned to the bungalow and became lost in wonder, as to why such an Alhambra of glory should have been permitted to sink into such night. But presently our reveries were broken by the bugle-call of the boatman, and we retraced our steps to the landing and were rowed back to Parkersburg in a skiff, which set forth the beauty of the Island from another angle. The view was magnificent, as the boat slowly withdrew to the head of this "gem on the fair bosom of the current," and disclosed the willow-fringed banks and forests. Small wonder that it caught the fancy of the Blenner-hassetts; and that it has held the attention of a world throughout the years, with such a halo of romance encircling its natural charm.

It belonged to Elijah Backus* at the time our story opens, and was known upon the maps as "Backus Island." The only building upon it at that time was the old blockhouse, built by Captain John James, near 1791, who came from Connecticut with the emigrant party to the mouth of the Muskingum, in 1790, and made a name for himself in Indian warfare. Hildreth, in his early Settlers of Ohio, tells us that this block-house stood just about a half-mile below the upper end of the Island. According to an excerpt, taken from a photostat copy of a letter, written February 21, 1798, by Colonel Israel Putnam, of Marietta to his son, David Putnam, at Plainfield, Connecticut, which is now in the Museum at Marietta, Blennerhassett built an addition to this blockhouse. It reads:

"An Irishman, located in England, said to be worth about 30-thousand dollars, has bought the upper part of Backus Island for $4,500 and is about building some addition to the blockhouse."

*See Continuous Ownership of Island for story of Backus.

Photo by Davies

The Old Neale Mansion as it Looks To-day

Photo by Davies

Amos K. Gordon, left, with a Group of Friends

2

The Island of To-day

But what shall we say of the Island of to-day? —1939, just one hundred and forty-two years, after the Blennerhassetts laid claim to its soil. It's doubtful if the park was ever more beautiful in its palmy days, with the touch of the lawnmower upon it now and its park of wonderful trees, so perfectly kept.

Since 1827 when George Neale II purchased the Blennerhassett tract, part of it has been in the Neale Family. Amos K. Gordon, his grandson, by inheritance and purchase gradually gained possession, and late in November, 1935, he bought the eighty-seven acres that had strayed from the estate, and thus became the sole owner. From that hour the improvement and restoration of the Island has gone forth steadily with telling effect.

The several farms of yesterday have been merged into one; the briery paths have disappeared; preservation work has been done on the old sycamore of Indian Times, and other trees, and new trees have been planted; a new Memorial Avenue, 2800 by 50 feet, has been laid out, extending from the woods to the old sycamore near the brick mansion, which is set apart for black walnut trees, and which is flanked by American Elms. The old brick mansion has been relieved of its tenants, and placed on the honor roll for preservation, with ornamental touches of landscaping about it. The old well still holds its interest and gives out its cooling waters to the thirsty; the small bungalow still marks the site of the court and mansion of other days—in short it is all here but the mansion, and it cannot be rebuilt until some plan of flood control is worked out; for the Island was twelve feet below water, 1937. Neither will it be a public park, but a "shrine sacred to history"—the dream of a lad as he lay under the great trees and looked up at the stars, when he played about his grandfather's plantation in the long ago—"a place to visit and go away with thoughtful memories."

3

Who was Harman Blennerhassett?

Blennerhassett was an old and honored name of English nobility. Robert Blennerhassett, who traced his lineage back to King John, of England, emigrated to Ireland, from the Cumberland, during the reign of Queen Elizabeth, and became the head of three highly-respected branches of Irish gentry. Conway Blennerhassett, his son, was the father of Harman Blennerhassett, who is so interesting to us.

Conway Blennerhassett, we are told, was a man of large fortune and corresponding influence. Harman Blennerhassett, the youngest son of this large family, was born on October 8, 1764 or 5, while his parents were on a visit with relatives at Hampshire, England. The event evidently escaped record at the time, for later in life while making notations in his diary on October 8, Harman says, "this day is my birthday," but he is uncertain as to just how old he is; as "my parents could never quite agree as to which year I was born."

According to custom the youngest son must be educated for a profession befitting the dignity of the ancient family name that he held, and Harman Blennerhassett, being the youngest of three sons and six daughters came under the mandates of this custom. The bar was at all

times a favored gateway to political preferment and
fortune, and naturally his parents selected this profession
for him. Following his preliminary education, he entered
the famous King's Inns, at Dublin, 1790, and came out
on November 18, 1795, with his law degree. In this
same class was Robert Emmett, the noted Irish patriot,
who was admitted to the bar at the same time.

There is nothing to indicate that Harman Blennerhassett was a brilliant scholar, though he may have
been a hard student. But his father and two elder
brothers were now dead, and he was advanced to the
head of the family with a rich heritage, which precluded
the necessity of his settling down to the practice of his
profession immediately, and he gratified his desire for
a tour of the Continent. His sisters were the wives of
men of title and influence and this brought him in
contact with the leading people of the hour, not only
in Ireland, but in England and Scotland, as well, and
he made the most of his opportunity. But Fate in her
decrees lay concealed along his pathway, and it was
while he was on this tour, 1796, that the incident was
enacted that wrote the prelude to the story of Blennerhassett Island, and to his own and many other lives.

While a guest at the home of Captain Robert Agnew,
the lieutenant-governor of the Isle of Man, Harman
Blennerhassett was sent across the English Channel to
accompany the daughter home from school. He was
now a man of thirty-one, and Margaret Agnew was a

beautiful girl of eighteen. He was so captivated by her grace and charm when he saw her that he seemed to forget the trust reposed in him, the purpose of his mission, and under the spell of the moment, persuaded her to marry him without delay. Margaret Agnew was, doubtless, not so unlike the girl of to-day, who listens to some wooing voice under the moonlight and takes this irrevocable step without consideration of its consequences. But the awakening came in the consternation that followed when they arrived at her home and announced the nuptials. The parental blessing was withheld; the marriage proved so distasteful to kith and kin in general that Blennerhassett soon made his decision to cast his lot in the wilds of Young America, where solace and promise beckoned.

Under the vehement protest of the family, he sold his estate in Ireland to Thomas Millin—later Lord Vinty—for $160,000, breaking the entail, and went to London where he purchased his library and other outfit; then with his beautiful bride, and a retinue of servants, set sail for the Western World, while the roses of May whispered of a haven of love and happiness somewhere beyond the sea. They sailed from Gravesend, England, on a merchant vessel bound for New York, and landed in that city on August 1, 1796, after an uneventful voyage of seventy-three days—the distance being increased to ten thousand miles by adverse winds, which carried them out of their course.

From Utretch, Long Island, he writes the above information under date of August 18, 1796, to his nephew, Thomas de Coursey, and continues:

"On first setting my foot on American soil, I was visited with sensations which I certainly never experienced in the old country." He dwells upon his regrets as he casts his eye upon the sea and remembers the vast distance between him and those he loves, but takes some comfort in the thought that "grand barriers" are also "between me and my enemies." He speaks of the ninety-six degrees of heat and of the uncomfortable visitations of the mosquitoes from the Jersey side. He spent some time in exploring Long Island, New York, New Jersey, and Philadelphia, but it was the country beyond the rugged Alleghenies that lured him on—the fertile valleys along the Ohio and the Mississippi of which he had heard much, that he must see for himself. So with his wife, he faced the perilous difficulties and crossed the mountains to Pittsburgh during the autumn of this year, and found his way to Marietta, Ohio by keelboat.

Through this solitude of forest and shadow, the Ohio wended its way to the "great Father of Waters." No steamer had yet ruffled its bosom, but its fertile lands surely invited cultivation. Here the graceful deer roamed undisturbed; the fox sought shelter where it would; the plaintive tones of the turtle dove, and the dismal howl of the hungry wolf, alike, echoed back from the distant hills, all of which were novel to the young lovers. Marietta at this time was the metropolis of the Buckeye State. Its people were kind and most hospitable to strangers. Its location was all that could be desired; so Blennerhassett cast anchor here for the winter. On one of these heights, he saw an ideal location for a castle of the Old World type, but its difficult ascent caused him to abandon the idea, and his eyes turned toward the Island, which he purchased in the spring.

4

The Island Purchased

This beautiful island seemed to be the climax of Blennerhassett's dream. In its picturesque settings in the close embrace of the silvery Ohio, it was surely one of Nature's fair jewels. Its majestic forest was still a stranger to the woodman's axe; its banks were bordered with willows whose drooping branches laved in the rippling waters; the brier and the woodbine entwined their tendrils about the underbrush; flowers of rare beauty native to the forest, sent forth their fragrance; and the little feathery songster made vocal these secluded groves, all of which lent irresistible charm to this wildwood for this man of Nature—this wanderer from another land. Could quiet and seclusion be nearer the ideal? could lovers be more completely lost to the outside world than in this sylvan retreat? Blennerhassett thought not, and in March, 1797, he purchased two hundred acres* of the island, more or less, of Elijah Backus for $4,500, removed to the old blockhouse with his wife, and began clearing for his planned castle.

Blennerhassett was evidently fond of display, and, if we may believe history and tradition, he carried out his desire to surpass with magical effect on this island. It was not long until the stranger descending the river

*See record description in later chapter.

beheld the outspread wings of a mansion, surrounded by graded lawns with green swards and waving elms, shrubbery, fruits, and flowers, in deft arrangement, with the forest in the background, which at once captivated the eye. Then there were thrifty orchards and gardens; walls covered by clambering honeysuckles and eglantine, which sent their sweet breath over other bowers of beauty in the center, and one hundred acres under cultivation with corn and other crops. The mansion was fifty-two by thirty feet with two stories and basement, and the rich furnishings within corresponded to the picturesque without. Its splendor when in its full sheen is best described by the silvery tongue of William Wirt :*

"A shrubbery, which Shenstone might have envied, blooms around him [Blennerhassett]; music that might have charmed Calypso and her nymphs is his; an extensive library spreads its treasures before him; a philosophical apparatus offers to him all the mysteries and secrets of nature; peace, tranquillity, and innocence shed their mingled delights around him; and to crown the enchantment, a wife, who is said to be lovely even beyond her sex, graced with every accomplishment that can render her irresistible, has blessed him with her love and made him the father of her children."

But to complete the picture at the time that this terrestrial paradise was at its zenith, one must catch a better glimpse of the Queen and the King of this realm.

*See Richmond trial for Wirt's description.

History and Tradition are a unit in their verdict that
Mrs. Blennerhassett was almost an ideal type of feminine grace and beauty. She is described as being tall
beyond the ordinary for her sex, well-formed, brilliant,
gracious and captivating in manner, with blue eyes that
sparkled with intelligence, as they looked out from
beneath long, brown lashes which hung like curtains
to conceal the depth of their loveliness. Her features
were of the Grecian mold; her complexion of the car-
nation hue in its naturaliness; and a colorful, silk Turkish turban usually concealed her luxurious brown hair.
Her superior mind had been cultivated to a remarkable
degree for one of her youth. She was not only well
educated in her native English, but spoke and wrote
both French and Italian; was a model housewife, a
skillful horsewoman; and a ruling spirit in the community. One writer thus concludes his eulogy:

"She was indeed a rich-souled creature in which the
first germ of womanhood had blossomed forth without
a weed to check or chill—to blight the growth. Like
Shakespeare's Portia when the blow fell, her loyalty for
her husband stood the test."

Turning to the King of the Realm, we do not find
so pleasing a personality. Blennerhassett was not the
beauideal type that at once commands the admiration
of the gentler sex, but on the contrary, he was rather
clumsy and awkward in bearing. Six feet in height,
slender and slightly stooped, and very near-sighted, is

the pen description that is left to us. But so far as books go, he was highly educated, and he handled the violin skillfully, sometimes playing his own composition. He usually wore a coat of blue broadcloth, with scarlet or buff-colored small clothes, silk hose, and shoes with silver buckles, but his appearance about home was on the careless. He loved the chase, but in his near-sightedness, his skill as a gunner has been preserved for our amusement. Peter, a domestic, was his attendant on these occasions; he would stand near his Master, and thus direct his movements: "Now level, Mr. Blen-nerhassett,—a little to the right, now to the left, steady, fire." Off would go the gun, they tell us, and not infrequently, the game, too.

This picture of wealth, taste, and apparent domestic peace and happiness will suffice for a glimpse of this Island Home when its fame began to be wafted on the wings of the winds, and discontent entered in. Three children, too, had been born in the meantime, but Margaret, the second, slipped away, at the end of two brief years, and Dominick and Harman, Jr., made up the household at this time.

5

Blennerhassett Meets Burr

It was springtime. The Ohio, stayed by its innumerable bends from an otherwise resistless torrent, rushed along at the swiftness of eight miles an hour for raft or craft. For hundreds of miles it coiled itself among lofty hills which sent their gurgling streamlets headlong into its basin below, and rippled by the narrow fringes of lowlands here and there which skirted its shores. May with her bowery wand had touched all nature with surpassing charm, and the Island home was never more bewitching in its enchantment.

One fair day a crude-looking ark or boat came floating down the current. That in itself could hardly have been an incident of more than passing notice, as the river craft was no uncommon means of travel at that early period, but that barque seemed freighted with ill-omen. It seemed to carry the very destiny of the fair Island in its hold, though none but Fate knew it; thus it lives in history.

A distinguished stranger high up in the councils of the nation occupied it. He had purchased it at Pittsburgh, a short time before for this special trip, at the nominal price of one hundred thirty-five dollars. His journal describes it as "A floating house sixty feet by fourteen, containing dining-room, kitchen with fireplace, and two bedrooms; roofed from stem to stern, steps to go up and a walk on top the whole length, glass windows, etc."

This boat left Pittsburgh on April 30, 1805 and stopped at Wheeling on May 3, so that its occupants could view that town, which was described in the journal of the trip as "A pretty, neat village well situated on the south bank [of the river], containing sixty or eighty houses." It reached Marietta, Ohio, on May 5 where a cordial reception was extended, and the historic mounds visited. This town is described as "containing about eighty houses, some that would be called handsome in any village on the continent." At nightfall this interesting craft landed at Blennerhassett Island, just as many other travelers did at seeing such a palace in the wilderness.*

The strangers were received with the usual hospitality of the Island, but the surprise of the Master and Mistress of the mansion can better be imagined than described when they learned that their guest was no other than a former vice president of the United States; for this was their introduction to Aaron Burr, who was to play such an all-important part in their future lives and in the destiny of the beloved Island; and his companion was Gabriel Shaw, of Pittsburgh.

The evening was spent pleasantly in general conversation, and the Host and Hostess were much impressed

*Taken from Burr's own Journal.

with the engaging manner and wit of Colonel Burr. When 11 o'clock came, he and his companion were invited to occupy the guest chamber for the night, but they courteously declined the invitation, though it was pressingly repeated, Colonel Burr preferring to sleep in his boat, as was his custom on these occasions, saying, "There is no society in sleep, and we will see you in the morning."

The evening was fine and Mr. and Mrs. Blennerhassett walked down to the river with them. As they approached the moorings, Burr's foot slipped and he fell. Immediately recovering himself, he exclaimed, "That's an ill-omen"! But they remained in the boat overnight, rejoined the Blennerhassetts at breakfast in the morning, and continued their tour on down the river either that day or the next.*

Aaron Burr had had numerous honors thrust upon him, but his star was glimmering in its Western horizon, as he sailed down the river revolving whatever plans he may have had for the future in his mind. When the door of the Senate chamber closed on Vice President Burr and left its occupants in tears, a little more than two months before, no one would have suspected that so gifted a person could have walked away to such a doom. But he turned from that Senate chamber a ruined man, financially, politically, and in reputation. The

*From description of that visit in own hand of Harman Blennerhassett II.

very men that he had helped to enthrone were combined for his ruin. His duel with Hamilton had ostracized him in the East, but dueling was not in disfavor in the West, and he was acclaimed somewhat as a conquering hero at Cincinnati and other points down the river.

At Fort Massac at the mouth of the Cumberland, he met with General Wilkinson with whom he had scaled the Heights of Abraham in Revolutionary days. Wilkinson was now in command of the Western troops of the United States Army, and had just been appointed as governor of the Louisiana territory for the purpose of settling the boundary line dispute with Spain. Burr, not realizing his unprincipledness, confided his plans of empire to him, and readily won his sanction and pledge of support. Burr, in speaking of this meeting with Wilkinson in his Journal says, "Here [at Fort Massac] found General Wilkinson on his way to St. Louis. The General and his officers fitted me out with an elegant barge, sails, colors, and ten oars, with sergeant and ten, able, faithful hands. Thus equipped I left Massac on the 10th of June. Arrived at Nachez on the 17th nearly eight hundred miles from Massac. Then to New Orleans, back to Nashville." He speaks repeatedly of the hospitality of the people, which detained him. "Hospitality to A. B. not to the Vice President."

Upon his return from this tour in October Burr again stopped at the Island, but Blennerhassett and his wife were not at home. He had been called to New York,

by the arrival of Thomas Addis Emmett, in the meantime, and Mrs. Blennerhassett accompanied him as far
as Baltimore where she remained with friends, and they
did not return until the latter part of December. Thus
they missed Burr on his second visit to the Island.

During this same month, December, Blennerhassett
received a letter from Burr expressing regret that his
absence had prevented the opportunity of his cultivating
a further personal acquaintance with him, but the letter
made no mention of the enterprise. Contrary to the
prevailing belief of a century, Blennerhassett in his
reply to this letter made the overtures in this step which
resulted so disastrously for him and the beautiful Island;
as his letter will testify:

Blennerhassett's letter to Burr* in part— December
21, 1805. "But the interests of a growing family, I
feel, will summon me again into active life, to the
resumption of my former profession of the bar, mercantile, or other enterprise, if I should find an opportunity of selling or letting my establishment here to a
gentleman who could, without sacrifice, give me a price
by which I should not lose too much of the money it
stands me in, say $50,000; or afford me a rent of $2,500,
which by proper management, it might be made to
realize without paying at the highest rate half the yearly
value of the extensive and numerous conveniences on

*See Appendix C in this volume for summary of Blenner-
hassett's Brief in Court.

the place, with a detail of which I forbear to trouble you, observing merely that there is now in good order, say, two hundred acres, which with twenty well managed hands employed in raising hemp would afford a handsome profit. In either way, if I could sell or lease the place, I would move forward with a firmer confidence in any undertaking which your sagacity might open to profit and fame.

"Having thus advised you of my desire and motives to pursue a change of life, to engage in anything which may suit my circumstances, I hope, sir, you will not regard it indelicate in me to observe to you how highly I should be honored in being associated with you in any contemplated enterprise you would permit me to participate in. The amount of means I could at first come forward with would be small. You might command my services as a lawyer, or in any other way you should suggest as being most useful. I could, I have no doubt, unite the talents and energy of two particular friends, who would share in any fortune which might follow you. The gentlemen alluded to are Mr. Dudley Woodbridge, junior, of Marietta; and Mr. Devereux, of Baltimore, a ci-devant-general in the Irish rebel army, either of whom, it is proper to remark, could be prevailed upon to enlist in the undertaking.

"Not presuming to know or to guess at the intercourse, if any, subsisting between you and the present government, but viewing the probability of a rupture with Spain, the claim for action the country will make upon your talents, in the event of an engagement against, or subjugation of, any of the Spanish territories, I am disposed, in the confidential spirit of this letter, to offer you my friends, and my own services to cooperate in any contemplated measures in which you may embark. In making this proposition, I hope, sir, you will feel that it flows in a conviction of your judgment and talents, from a quarter that ever did and always will prefer to seek fortune and fame through the call, rather than the coercion, of any government.

"A further development of my views would at present aggravate the trespass on your time by this letter, too much prolonged, and would besides, I hope, be a guarantee of the perfect confidence you may repose in my integrity in any communication you may be pleased to honor me with.

"I shall await with much anxiety the receipt of your reply, and with warm interest in your success and prosperity."

It was several months before Burr replied to this letter and he did not then encourage Blennerhassett's hopes. He admitted to having an enterprise in mind, "but the business, however, depends in some degree on contingencies not within my control, and it will not be commenced before December or January, if ever. But I must insist that these intimations be not permitted to interrupt the prosecution of any plans which you have formed for yourself." He goes so far as to suggest New Orleans if Blennerhassett wishes to leave his scenes of enchantment, and says, "As a place of business it offers great advantages; most of those who style themselves lawyers are become visionary speculators, or political fanatics."

But this correspondence finally brought Burr to the Island in August, 1806, in company with his confidential friend, Colonel de Pestre, and it was at this time that the plans were outlined for the expedition. According to Blennerhassett's brief in court, Burr remained over night and together they went to Marietta where they hurriedly made a contract with Dudley Woodbridge, who had been for years the business partner of Blennerhassett, for the construction of the boats; after first entering into an agreement for advance funds with Mr. Alston, as surety for Blennerhassett, upon the recommendation of Burr that Alston was one of the wealthiest men in America.

Plans now went rapidly forward. Blennerhassett had charge of the construction of the boats, and Burr was constantly on the wing in the interest of financial aid, "throwing out his bait where there were any fish to bite." He had enlisted wealth and influence and the autumn found the details well in hand. He came and went from the Island, and his daughter spent much time there during the season of preparation for the journey. She and Mrs. Blennerhassett were kindred souls

in talent and culture, and they were the animating
spirits of the enterprise in their cheeriness and glee. One
boat had been tastefully fitted out for the use of the
family.

But somehow Blennerhassett could not quiet his
apprehensions. While he admitted that he did not fully
understand the enterprise, his confidence in Burr's
judgment and honor led him on. He wanted to draw
out public sentiment on the question of the separation
of the Atlantic States from the rest, and contributed a
series of articles to the Ohio State Journal under the
name of "Querist"* on the subject for the purpose of
calling forth expression. Then in October, 1806, in
order to satisfy himself as to Burr's purpose and progress,
he made a trip to Lexington, Kentucky where he remained for more than two weeks as an observer of Burr's
growing popularity. But notwithstanding his observa-
tions, Blennerhassett received a message from home
which served to increase rather than allay his fears. This
message was to the effect that the people of Wood County
had been in communication with the President and
with the Governor of Virginia in regard to their alarm
over this movement; that a volunteer battalion of three
companies, which had been organized and armed by
the militia, was under general muster; and that the
feeling against him and Burr warranted fear of violence.

*See "Life of John Marshall," by Beveridge, volume 3,
page 311, for comment on Querist; also Appendix B for
Henderson Depositions.

Blennerhassett now quickened his homeward footsteps, arriving on November 3 to find the situation one of gravity, indeed. In the meantime Mrs. Blennerhassett had received assurance from Colonel Phelps, which somewhat quieted his fears; gave him courage to talk the matter over with Colonel Phelps, and to ask him to invest in the land enterprise.

But the excitement was not to be easily calmed. Daily rumors of the destruction of the boats, and of the invasion of the Island did not serve to raise the drooping spirits of the troubled man, who feared for the safety of his family, as well as for his own. So his thoughts turned toward preparation for withdrawal. But he solicited no one, neither did he offer inducement or wages, but instructed those who wished to accompany him to provide for themselves rifles and blankets. No implements of war, no military stores were to be included.

But despite Blennerhassett's efforts to quiet the fears of his neighbors, while he prepared for departure, the discussions pro and con over the legitimacy of the movement went right on. Burr's intimacy with the British Minister, and the building of the boats in such a remote region served to increase suspicion. And in the midst of this dilemma, a letter came from Burr telling of his arrest, trial, and release in Kentucky, which must delay the plans of settlement.

Trouble now seemed to loom up on every hand. Whis-

pers of suspicion, without evidence to confirm, were
borne upon the very wings of the winds; warnings were
sent out to officials to be on the lookout for a military
expedition, but nothing of the sort was visible, it seemed.
True, these boats had been seen by the authorities, but
they were just frail, harmless-looking things, manned by
a half-dozen men each, without the slightest claim to
military status, and the people along the Ohio and the
Mississippi were mystified, as to what the ado was
all about.

General Wilkinson might have explained, as he
without doubt, held the key to the entire situation, but
he was too busy in other directions just now. Burr's
famous cipher letter had reached him by special messenger at Natchez on October 8, with its request for General
Wilkinson to be ready to join him and march with him
to New Orleans. But things of great importance had
taken place since that agreement had been made. The
Prime Minister of England, who had pledged support
to the enterprise, was now dead, and his successor was
not in sympathy with his policy. War with Spain was
no longer imminent, and other potent factors had been
withdrawn. General Wilkinson must save himself by
disavowing his part in the enterprise, at whatever cost
to Burr; and his innate cowardice and duplicity now
asserted itself. He suddenly turned "patriot and rescuer
of his country," and his activity knew no bounds.

The bearer of the cipher letter was graciously received,

but was detained in camp for ten days, while all possible concerning Burr's plans was learned from him. A messenger was then dispatched to Washington with a complete betrayal of trust. "The treasonable movement on foot" was startlingly announced; warning was sent to the Commander at New Orleans to fortify for defense for hostilities looked certain; General Wilkinson then marched his army to the Sabine and back, and sent it to New Orleans under Colonel Cushing. While rushing around smartly, on November 7, he wrote an officer, "I perceive the plot thickens. Yet all but those concerned sleep profoundly. My God! what a situation has our country reached? Let us save it if we can . . . if I mistake not, we shall have an insurrection of blacks, as well as whites, to combat . . . Hurry, hurry after me, and if necessary, let us be buried together in the ruins of the place we shall defend." Now it occurs to him to carry the ruse further, and on November 12, he sends a warning to Governor Claiborne of the "dangers ahead of which he has not yet dreamed"; and suggests that the storm will likely break forth in New Orleans "where I shall meet it and triumph or perish." He further says that "within six days the President will be fully apprised of the plot which implicates thousands."*

Suffice it to say that in accord with General Wilkinson's well laid plan, the President's proclamation was

*1—*Wilkinson to Cushing, November 7, 1806, " Wilkinson Memoirs"; also Beveridge's "Life of John Marshall," Volume 3, page 330.*

forthcoming on November 27, two days after the arrival of the messenger from him. With all this volume of information to the President, it seemed strange that General Wilkinson "did not know who was concerned"; nor that he did not think it worth while to send Burr's cipher letter. That President Jefferson should have issued such a proclamation on a mass of unconvincing reports from one individual, alone, is short of amazing, but the indisputable fact remains that he did, and history is not silent on the personal motive behind it.

The proclamation designated "sundry persons conspiring and confederating together to begin a military expedition or enterprise against the dominions of Spain," though it seems all knew where to look for the "sundry" individuals. These persons were ordered to withdraw their activities, and the civil and military officials were authorized to "be vigilant and to seize all boats and supplies, to give information, and to apprehend the guilty." General Wilkinson, also, received instructions from the Secretary of War authorizing him to exert his power. New pledges of fidelity to the government were required; and all the while General Wilkinson grew more and more excited over the impending danger.

His stories were a bit at variance, and he occasionally found it necessary to write the President in protest of his loyalty, lest his faith in him be shaken by the accusations against him. At times he was almost pathetic in his zeal and innocence. But this ruse must be kept going. In the meantime, he blew into New Orleans and began a reign of lawless violence, which, according to Beveridge's "Life of John Marshall," has no parallel in American history. Men of prominence were arrested and thrown into prison; and some of them were sent to Washington to be released by the Chief Justice of the United States, who, as opposed to the Chief Magistrate, could discover no act of treason in them. But Wilkinson had overplayed his ruse in the Crescent City and by and by the people began to recover from the fright, and to see the amusing side. In this crisis it became necessary to discredit either Wilkinson or Burr. The cipher letter now found its way to the President and to the press in what later proved to be the Wilkinson version.

In the meantime John Graham* had been appointed secretary of the Orleans territory for the purpose of investigating the activities of Burr, as warnings had been reaching the President, who paid no heed until the Wilkinson maneuvers began. From Pittsburgh Graham dropped down the river to Marietta and saw the boats in building at the mouth of the Muskingum, and found Blennerhassett open and frank about the expedition to the Bastrop's lands. He visited General Neville, the Morgans, and the Hendersons, who were not friendly to Blennerhassett; and wrote Mr. Madison on November 28 from Chillicothe, Ohio, that all was

*See McCaleb, pages 203-4, for Graham version, and 225-26 same volume.

quiet; that the people "at this place seem to know nothing
of the plans of Burr, and I am rather induced to think
that he has no one at work for him here." But to Governor Tiffin of Ohio, he told quite a different story. However incredible this may have sounded to the Governor
at first, as he knew that these boats were too frail for
military purposes and insisted so, on December 2, we
find him telling the legislature what this "respectable
gentleman in U. S. cloth and public character" has
told him concerning the expedition for the purpose of
"seizing New Orleans, etc." Four days later he is
authorized by that legislature to call out the militia;
and this Ohio militia took its place along the river on
December 10, as a result of John Graham's zeal. Fifteen
boats in their varied states of completion, and two hundred barrels of provision were seized at the mouth of
the Muskingum and at Marietta, and Graham went
quietly on his way to Kentucky to see what other "duty"
he might perform.

A local report of this act which scarcely veils its
derision has been preserved for our amusement. It
reads:

"A warlike array of undisciplined militia with can-
non, necessary equipage and arms, stationed themselves
along the banks of the river to cut off forces expected
from above. Many amusing jokes were got off at the
expense of the raw recruits during this campaign, such
as setting an empty tar barrel on fire and placing it in

an old boat or raft of logs to float in the darkness of night. The sentries after duly hailing and receiving no answer would fire a shot to enforce their commands; but still dead silence reigned, and calmly the phantom vessel with her stolid crew floated onward and downward in utter recklessness and indifference. Irritated at such manifest contempt of their high authority, they plunged into the stream to seize its luckless navigators when 'confusion utterly confounded' nothing appeared but the remains of a log and barrel, which some laughter-loving wag had freighted for their mischance and his own amusement. Pranks of this sort were nightly played on those reluctant defenders of the Union.''

Blennerhassett knew that the Wood County Militia was planning to invade the Island; and that it was being watched from both sides, though the boats still passed down the current, and he was much alarmed as he feared arrest. Comfort Tyler, who had served in the legislature of New York with Burr, and Israel Smith with their four boats and thirty-two settlers for the new colony, stopped on their way down the river on December 10, and Blennerhassett no longer hesitated in his decision that safety lay in flight.

6

The Flight from the Island

It was a busy scene at the mansion when the Master finally determined on flight. Fires were burning; lanterns waving; and feet flying in the darkness, as the stores and supplies were transferred to the waiting boats. It was midnight on December 10 when the last trunk left the hall, and a cold drizzle of rain added its chill to the inky darkness, as the little party made its way from the mansion to the footway of rails at the bottom of the bank which led to the boat.

Mrs. Blennerhassett, Mr. and Mrs. McCastle, who were guests at the mansion, and General Edward Tupper, who had arrived about 11 o'clock for the purpose of collecting some money from Mr. Blennerhassett, accompanied him to the river. Owing to the uncertain walking in the rain, Mrs. Blennerhassett took leave of her husband at the footway. General Tupper stood near her watching those going aboard by the light of the lanterns, and, from his deposition which was found long years after in Ohio, "there was no arrest, and no warlike evidence in this assemblage on this night." He expressed the hope that Mr. Blennerhassett would make no resistance in case attempts to arrest him were made; and received the assurance that he would not in the following language: "We shall surrender ourselves

The old well as it appears to-day, and view of the lawn

Mrs. Blennerhassett's Flight from the Island

to the civil authority whenever it shall present itself; for our object is both lawful and honorable as respects the United States." At this Mr. Tyler remarked that they were not in a position to defend themselves, if they were so disposed, with but four or five guns, some pistols and dirks on board; but that they would, however, defend themselves as best they could against unauthorized attempts to molest them. So this story which comes from the family papers, sets aside the one of arrest, the snowstorm, and others which have gone before.

Mrs. Blennerhassett now bade her husband adieu, and with her guests returned to the mansion. The next morning, December 11, the boats were gone, and on the 18th they joined Burr at the mouth of the Cumberland.

On this same morning, December 11, Mrs. Blennerhassett went to Marietta to secure the boat that had been prepared for the family in order that she might follow her husband, but she learned to her great disappointment of the seizure of the boats and the supplies.

Returning to the Island, she was confronted by a state of lawlessness and general disorder. Under the President's Proclamation, Colonel Phelps had taken possession that morning shortly after her departure, and finding it deserted, he, with part of his men, had gone overland hoping to intercept the flotilla along the river. During his absence under the exhilarating influence of the tempting wines of the well-stored cellar, the moblike spirit of the militia ran riot. The fences were destroyed by the fires of the sentinels; the shrubbery, trampled under reckless feet; the mansion ransacked by vandal hands, and the elegant apartments, turned into barracks. Mrs. Blennerhassett was met by insult, and her servants were frightened away. Colonel Phelps offered apologies and threw every possible protection about her upon his return that evening, but there seemed little that could be done under such deplorable circumstances.

Another incident of the day, which added color to the riotous scene, was the arrival of fourteen young adventurers under Morgan Neville* from Pittsburgh, who were volunteers for the Burr expedition. They had been arrested by the Wood county authorities and sent to the Island for trial which was turned into a farce and they were set free.

Under these difficulties, the prospect for joining her husband did not look encouraging to Mrs. Blennerhassett, but one of these young men offered her a room in his boat with as much comfort as it would afford, and she gladly accepted. Preparations for flight now took on renewed vigor, and Colonel Phelps courteously rendered all the assistance possible to lighten her task.

It was December 17 when this fateful little craft, lashed to another of its class, swung from shore. She who had been the presiding genius of this fair Island

*See affidavit of Neville, page 97.

home for eight years now plunged into the darkness never again to know happiness. It was a bleak day when she set sail with her two little sons in this cabin flatboat through the ice. Missing her husband at the mouth of the Cumberland, she followed on into the more rapid current of the "Father of Waters," where she joined him at his moorings at the entrance of Bayou Pierre on January 24, 1807. Under this date, we find this notation in Blennerhassett's Journal, "The Family arrived today at 3 o'clock p. m. in the boat of Thomas Butter, who was on his way from Pittsburgh and called to take my family on board at the Island." So it is left for us to conjecture whether Thomas Butter was really one of the young adventurers or not, as he stops at this; but we see that she was more than a month in reaching him.

By this time the joy of reunion was overcast by apprehension, which daily became more haunting. While Burr and his expedition had been placidly making their way down the Ohio and the Mississippi, all unconscious of the gathering tempest, Wilkinson had been "saving the Republic" by rending its laws at New Orleans, and sending Burr's messengers as prisoners on the high seas under charge of treason. But on January 10, 1806, while Burr was ashore at the home of a friend at Bayou Pierre, near Natchez, he learned with consternation of Wilkinson's betrayal; that he was considered as a traitor by the Mississippi authorities; and that the whole country

was aroused over his movement. The cipher* letter (in
the Wilkinson version of course) had already appeared
in the press. This was a stunning blow. He went back
to his boats and shifted them to the other side, outside
the jurisdiction of the Mississippi territory, and encamped himself with sentinels on guard. Dismay now
settled down over the spirits of the young adventurers
of the expedition when they learned that they were
considered traitors, rebels against their government;
for they were mostly mere youth who had no conception
of anything wrong, and such a charge was overwhelming
to their loyalty. When Blennerhassett, Tyler, and Floyd,
with their parties joined Burr at the mouth of the Cumberland on a little island and lined up in a semi-circle,
so that each might meet Colonel Burr, he did not reveal
the purpose of the expedition, but promised to do so
later.

However, Burr in this dilemma immediately issued
a public statement protesting against such a charge, and
inviting investigation, as his boats were "merely the
vehicles of immigration." This brought officials to his
encampment. On Janury 17, he met the Acting Governor
of Mississippi and voluntarily submitted his boats to
the civil authorities, and they were searched without
discovery of military armament. [Here is where the
story of his having sunk his arms at night just in time
to save himself, comes in; but this story cannot be

*See text of Cipher letter, Appendix D.

substantiated unless we go into the vernacular of General Wilkinson and his plotters]. It was at this time that Cowles Meade* wrote the government that "with all its exaggerations, there were but nine boats and one hundred men, the major part of which are boys and young men just from school, who were evidently ignorant of Colonel Burr's designs—evidently dupes, if Generals Eaton, and Wilkinson are to be accredited." Seven days after Burr left Fort Massac, Captain Bissel, in reply to a letter of inquiry from Andrew Jackson, assured him that "nothing the least alarming had appeared; that Burr had passed with a few boats having nothing on board that would even suffer a conjecture more than a man bound to market. The boats were comfortable, much like the modern houseboat." John Murrell, of Tennessee, who had been delegated on a secret mission of investigation, reported to Andrew Jackson that he had closely followed Burr, and that there were but ten boats with sixty men on board and no appearance of arms. Burr was totally unequipped for anything but settlement, and poorly for that. The Acting Governor of Mississippi, according to Beveridge in the "Life of John Marshall," winds up his comment on the situation as follows: "Thus sir this mighty alarm, with all its exaggeration, has eventuated in nine boats and one hundred men [1000 had been reported] and the major

*See Beveridge's version of this in "Life of John Marshall," Volume 3, pages 362-68 and McCaleb's, pages 172-74.

part of these are boys or young men just from school who are wholly unaware of Burr's designs."

Returning to the court proceedings, it was on February 2 that Burr appeared before the Judges of the Supreme Tribunal of the Territory. He made a most favorable impression on their honor, but they decided that the case did not come under their jurisdiction, and it was turned over to the grand jury, where again "no fault was found" in Burr. On the contrary the matter was treated humorously. But instead of being released Burr was required to report to court the next day and the next without any reason; and on February 4, he asked to be released from his bond only to be refused by Judge Rodney, who gave no explanation for his action, though the grand jury had vindicated. Burr's friends now became alarmed, as they suspected a Wilkinson accomplice in the Judge, and they advised him to conceal himself for safety. Governor Williams had returned in the meantime, and had manifested signs of hostility toward the Colonel, and it later developed that Wilkinson was behind the scenes with a kidnapping scheme which boded bodily harm to Burr.

However, on February 5, the Colonel did not appear in court, and the Governor's Proclamation for his arrest and a reward of two thousand dollars for his capture was forthcoming on the following day. From his place of concealment, Burr notified Governor Williams that he was ready to submit himself whenever his citizen's rights were guaranteed; and, a few days later, again reminded the Governor that he was only bound by law to appear in case an indictment should be found. But this did not seem to matter, he was still considered as a fugitive and he knew what to expect—a court-martial from the Judas who had betrayed him.

In secret he visited his boats and took leave of the men, who were to keep the barges and to go on to the Bastrop lands if they chose or sell them and divide the spoils. He was compelled to flee from persecution. But none of the men had the heart to go on now. Some of them were arrested on the suspicion aroused by a spurious note purporting to be from Burr to them, after his disappearance, but they were all released but Blennerhassett, Tyler, Floyd, and Ralston, who were held until April before they were finally set free. Many of the younger ones scattered through the Territory, supplied the schools with teachers, and entered various other professions. Most of them never knew what it was all about.

It was surely a dilemma, especially for the Blennerhassetts, who had never known hardships, but this proved to be just a mere incident in the long chain of disasters that was to follow.

Wilkinson was frantic lest Burr escape. Every effort was made to seize him; officers in disguise were sent to capture him, and men armed with dirks and pistols were dispatched to assassinate him.

While all this excitement was going on over Burr's expedition in the South, it is interesting to turn to the National Capital and catch a glimpse of some of the deliberations there. There were men in the United States Senate who shook their heads in skepticism over the rumors. Senator Plumer* in a letter to Jeremiah Mason on January 4, 1807, expresses his doubt thus:

"We have been and still are both amused and perplexed with the rumors, reports, and conjectures respecting Aaron Burr. They are numerous, various, and contradictory. . . . I must have plenary evidence before I believe him capable of committing the tenth part of the foolish and absurd things that are ascribed to him."

John Adams† writes to an intimate friend at this time:

"I never believed him [Burr] to be a Fool. But he must be an idiot or a lunatic, if he has really planned and attempted to execute such a project as is imputed to him. Politicians have no more regard for Truth than the Devil. . . . But if his guilt is as clear as the Noonday Sun, the first Magistrate ought not to have pronounced it so before a Jury had tried him."

Even Burr's enemies doubted the accuracy of Wilkinson's reports, and the version of his dispatch.

*Plummer Mss. in Library of Congress.

†Old Family letters; also see footnote page 338, Volume 3, "Life of John Marshall," Beveridge.

Windy Hill Manor

Photo taken by Paul Woodard
Windy Hill Manor, 1935

7

Burr's Capture and Journey to Richmond

Few phases of this interesting drama are more spectacular than Burr's capture and journey to Richmond; for no where else are his iron will and dogged determination more disclosed than in this dark hour, which robbed him of his honors; branded him as a traitor; and hurled him headlong into the yawning abyss of humiliation and despair.

After his escape from the Mississippi authorities, he returned to Windy Hill Manor where one of Colonel Osmen's best mounts awaited him, and where he found his close friend, Chester Ashley, ready to go with him. He was in the shabby guise of a boatman, we are told. His garb consisted of coarse, copperas-dyed, cloth trousers, an inferior, drab roundabout, and an ancient pattern of beaver hat, once white, with a broad, flapping brim. They were bound for the coast where Colonel Burr may have hoped to escape by sea, and they set out on this perilous journey under cover of darkness.

But if we may once again credit Tradition, the Colonel found a fair one in his pathway at Half Way Hill, soon after his departure, and, in accord with his weakness, lingered over the charms of this beautiful "Maid of Half Way Hill" until almost dawn, before he could pull himself away; thus wasting precious hours and hazarding his escape. This fair Madeline lived with her widowed mother in a vineclad cottage, and was a veritable Madonna in his eyes. He besieged her to become his wife and flee with him, but no! she could not go with him, but she readily yielded him her heart, as all other women seemed to do, and promised to wait for his return. But he never came. She waited long, and finally he wrote releasing her, and she then married another.

After this little episode, they pushed on through forest and swollen stream, losing their way, and thus encountering dangerous delay. Finally, late on the evening of February 18, they rode up to a house at Wakefield, Washington County, Alabama, and inquired the way to the home of Colonel Hinson whom Burr had met at Natchez and promised to visit. Their inquiry was answered by one Colonel Nicholas Perkins, who was standing near the village tavern, and who gave a very unfavorable report of the route, especially for strangers at this late hour of night. But they galloped off into the darkness unheedingly, and Colonel Perkins' suspicions began to stir. The manner and garb of the one in the flapping hat were so at variance; the lateness of the hour; and their unwillingness to be deterred by distance or bad roads, added to his perplexity; so he went to the home of the sheriff, imparted his suspicions, and induced him to rise from his bed and to go in pursuit with him; for we remember there was a two-thousand-dollar reward. They went, and the story generally accepted in the contradictions is as follows:

It was nearing the midnight hour when a glimmering light through the trees directed Burr and his Companion to the Hinson home. Their hail brought no response, and they dismounted and entered the kitchen where they soon rekindled the slumbering embers into flame. Burr had just settled down to comfort, while his Companion went to look after the horses, when another stranger entered. Mrs. Hinson, being alone, in the absence of her husband, had remained silent and out of sight until she recognized the voice of Sheriff Brightwell, her cousin; she then entered from another room, and at once began making preparations for something for her unexpected guests to eat.

Colonel Perkins, remembering that the stranger in the flapping hat had seen him at the log tavern, decided it better for him to remain outside, while Sheriff Brightwell got his impressions as to the possible identity of the stranger; and they were to meet at an appointed place in the woods, later.

Supper was now served, and Burr most courteously thanked his hostess for her kindness, with an apology for this extra trouble, as he took his seat at the table. His conversation was so brilliant that Mrs. Hinson, too, soon observed how little affinity there was between the manner of the man and his garb. Sheriff Brightwell stood before the fire an intent listener. By and by in a momentary absence of the stranger, at the suggestion of Brightwell, she asked his companion if she did not have the honor of entertaining Colonel Burr, but he in his confusion did not reply. However, the following morning, Burr disclosed to her his identity; expressed regret at the absence of her husband, and told her that he must be off, since his identity had been suspected. He inquired about the route he should take, wrote some letters, and departed.

For some reason not yet explained, Brightwell failed to return to Perkins, who remained shivering in the cold until his patience was exhausted, and then proceeded to Fort Stoddart, where he arrived, after some difficulty, early the next morning. He related his experience of the night before with his attendant suspicions to Commander Edward P. Gaines of the Fort, and plans were immediately laid for pursuit. With Lieutenant Gaines in charge of a file of soldiers, accompanied by Colonel Perkins, they set out, and soon met the man in the queer garb and flapping hat, with his traveling companion, and Sheriff Brightwell. Lieutenant Gaines in approaching him, said, "I presume I have the honor of addressing Colonel Burr?" He replied, "I am a traveler in a strange land, and do not recognize your right to ask such a question." Gaines then said, "I arrest you at the instance of the United States." "By what authority do you arrest me, a stranger, on the highway about my own private business?" came the retort. Gaines then told him that he was an officer of the United States Army, and that he held in his hand the proclamation of the President, as well as that of the Governor of the Mississippi territory, directing his arrest. Burr still protested, but was taken into custody, however, and all returned to Fort Stoddart, where he was assigned to an apartment with the assurance that all respect would be shown him, so long as he did not try to escape.

Perkins returned to Wakefield and brought about the arrest of Major Ashley, his traveling companion, but the Major escaped the guards and made his way to Tennessee and later proved valuable to Burr by collecting evidence in his behalf for the trial.

Finally, after much delay, arrangements were completed for Burr's removal from Fort Stoddart, and he was taken under guard in a government boat up the Alabama river and into the Tensaw Lake by Lieutenant Gaines, who stopped with him at the home of John Mills. Seeing the straits to which the Prisoner had been reduced, the women here wept in sympathy. At the boatyard in what is now Baldwin County, Alabama, the crew disembarked, and Gaines placed Colonel Perkins in charge. Perkins selected his guards from men that he knew could be depended upon. These men were pledged to hold no intercourse with the Prisoner, nor suffer him to escape alive. For Perkins was aware of the peculiar fascination of the man and feared the effect of close contact with the guards; thus he took every precaution to avoid it.

The party now proceeded on horseback, following the Indian trail from the Bigbee settlement to Fort Wilkinson. Burr still wore his home-spun garb and flapping hat, which were in striking contrast with the elegant manner in which he bestrode his fine steed; and his bearing would have graced the head of any regiment, however distinguished. All were mounted, with pistols in holsters. The one tent was pitched at night for the Prisoner, who lay down upon blankets before a blazing fire which sent its flickering shadows over dismal forests of impenetrable pines, which were haunted by wild beasts and savage Indians. There lay this brilliant man, who once lacked but one vote of the highest honor within the gift of his countrymen, stripped of all his glory; fortune gone, hopes crushed, hunted and slandered, even forbidden to write to the daughter he idolized. An ordinary individual could not have borne it, yet he rose in the morning, ate his breakfast and cheerfully resumed his journey; for days the rain fell in torrents; they were compelled to swim swollen streams, and were often drenched. Burr was a good horseman, and there was never a murmur from him about fatigue, though they traveled at the rate of forty miles a day.

At Fort Wilkinson, they found the first ferry on the whole route, and a few miles ahead, they rested beneath the first roof of civilization in a public house kept by one Mr. Bevin. Here the first noteworthy incident of the journey was enacted. Bevin, like most of the settlers along these highways, naturally inquired from whence they came? and when they replied "Bigbee Settlement" he immediately began plying questions concerning the traitor, Aaron Burr, suggesting that he must be a very bad man, wasn't people afraid of him? had he been caught yet?" etc. to the great annoyance of Perkins and his men. Burr was sitting in the corner by the fire with his head down, and finally when he could bear no more, he raised himself up and with flashing eye fixed on his host, said, "I am Aaron Burr, what is it you want with me?" The keenness of his eye, his agitation of manner, and his striking appearance, had its effect. The astonished host trembled like a leaf and talked no more while the party remained.

Shortly after they had crossed into South Carolina, another incident occurred at the small town of Chester where a group stood about a tavern, listening to dancing and music. Burr seeing hope of escape, for he realized that he had friends in the South, and that this state was the home of his beloved daughter, dismounted and exclaimed, "I am Aaron Burr under military arrest, and I claim protection of the civil authorities!" Perkins, who had already drawn the guard closer about the Prisoner when they entered South Carolina, leaped from his horse and ordered him to remount. "I will not!" Burr excitedly exclaimed. Not wishing to shoot him,

Perkins threw down his pistols, and, being a man of great physical strength, seized him about the waist and replaced him in the saddle, while one of the guards slipped the rein over the horse's head and led him away before the astonished citizens had time to realize what was taking place. Burr was in a high tension of excitement and gave way to tears, as did the kind-hearted Thomas Malone, one of the guards. This was the first time that anyone had ever seen Aaron Burr unmanned, and it must have been pathetic to see him yield to uncontrollable despondency.

The guards in their alarm suggested a carriage for the rest of the journey; Perkins acted upon this suggestion, and there was no further trouble.*

When they reached Richmond, the women were not long in providing the comforts that the Prisoner needed. Burr soon lost his shabby garb and was once again presentable in his accustomed style of raiment. It was March 26 when they arrived at the Eagle Tavern at Richmond, and Perkins went on to Washington to receive his two thousand dollar reward, and the thanks of the President, but returned to Richmond to give his testimony, which is still on record.

But let us return to Blennerhassett, who had thought that he was free from further trouble when he was released in the Mississippi territory. In June he set out

*See Picket's "History of Alabama," as best Authority for this story; also Appendix A.

Caps to Old Gateway

Photo by Davies

View of Old Sycamore as it Looks To-day

for the island, but was taken into custody at Lexington, Kentucky, for the endorsement of Burr's bills. He was trying to adjust this matter, which had not yet been settled, when he was indicted for treason at Richmond, and his arrest followed on July 21. Henry Clay was retained as his counsel, and letters from the Richmond Penitentiary conveyed this dreadful news to Mrs. Blennerhassett, whose loyal, courageous letter in such a trying hour may be found in the Blennerhassett Papers to-day.

Burr suggested that Blennerhassett send his wife and children to Theodosia. The women were devoted to each other, but Mrs. Blennerhassett evidently saw something in Mr. Alston that she did not like, and she refused to go. She asks her husband to tell Colonel Burr that if Mrs. Alston alone was in the question, "I would now this moment take refuge with her, and that I should not think my life even worth its present value, did I not hope once more to see and converse with that woman whom I think almost above human nature; but at the same time I would do nothing that might lessen the dignity of the attachment I feel for her."

8

Arraignment and Indictment

The preliminary hearing took place at the Eagle Tavern, at Richmond on March 30, 1807. Major Perkins was the chief verbal witness and he made the most of his opportunity to tell of the part that he had played in the capture, which was somewhat at variance with the one already recited in a preceding chapter. He omitted the Sheriff Brightwell incident, and he, himself, went into the Hinson home, where he intently eyed the stranger in the queer garb, who seldom spoke, acted as if he did not care to be observed, and glanced his way but once. When he had concluded Chief Justice Marshall adjourned the hearing to the Capitol for the following day, and released the Prisoner under a bond of five thousand dollars.

But at the reconvening on March 31, the throng was so great that the session was adjourned to the chamber of the house of delegates. The affidavits of Generals Wilkinson and Eaton entered in and they were dramatic tales of alleged revelations of Burr's perfidy and treason. General Eaton's not only confirmed the conspiracy story to destroy the Union, but disclosed the horrifying one of his intentions to assassinate the President. Mr. Wickham contended that there was no evidence of treason against the Prisoner, and Colonel Burr finally

rose and asked to be permitted to state a few facts;
namely, That warrant had been issued upon mere
conjecture; that alarm existed without cause; that Wilkinson had alarmed the President, and that the President
had alarmed the people along the Ohio. He appealed
to historical facts: In each case when he had learned of
the suspicions surrounding his movements that he had
paused and invited investigation—in Kentucky, in
Tennessee, and in the Mississippi Territory—and in
each case had been vindicated and discharged; that these
facts, alone, should overthrow this testimony against
him. He insisted that his motive was honorable, and
that it would have proved helpful to the United States.
His flight had been held as an evidence of his guilt and
he asked at what time did he fly? Not until he had been
acquitted and promised the protection of the Government—a protection which could not be performed—did
he fly, because bodily safety demanded it. He further
asked as to why the guard, who conducted him to
that place, avoided every magistrate on the way? unless
for the conviction that such action was without authority. Why had he been denied the use of pen, ink, and
paper, and the right to send a letter to his own daughter?
In support of the truthfulness of Colonel Burr's statements, at this point, let us read the verdict of the Kentucky jury on December 5, 1806, for ourselves:

"The grand jury are happy to inform the court that

no violent disturbance of the public tranquility or breach of the law, has come to their knowledge."*

However, Colonel Burr's pleadings were in vain, but the Chief Justice, in firm, but gentle tones refused to insert the charge of high treason in the commitment and made it misdemeanor only. The bond was now changed to ten thousand dollars, and the case was set for May 22, 1807, at the next term of the court for the district of Virginia.

President Jefferson was inconsolable over the ruling of the Chief Justice, as this was a blow to the prosecution at the outset, for the Government must sustain its case after all this Wilkinson bluster or become an object of ridicule for a "much-ado-about-nothing." From this moment, John Marshall, too, was on trial, and history justifies the assertion that President Jefferson, Wilkinson, and others high up in the councils of the Nation, occupied like positions.

Court convened on May 22. The grand jury† was finally empaneled with John Randolph, jr. as foreman, and several future statesmen included in its personnel. It was without doubt one of the most distinguished juries that has ever been recorded in history. General Wilkinson was the star witness to be sure, but it was not until June 13 that he arrived, along with John

---

*See Appendix A. Henry Clay on effect of this verdict in Courtroom.

†See names of the sixteen in appendix E.

Graham, and Lieutenant Gaines. The appearance of this "gigantic accomplisher of all things whose torch was to kindle the fatal blaze" was a matter of no small moment. Betting had been going on about the taverns and at the corner boxes on the streets that Burr would decamp at the appearance of this all-important witness. But let us permit Washington Irving to describe this interesting scene upon the entrance of General Wilkinson to the court room on June 15.

He first speaks in his letter of the wagers that Burr would decamp, and then continues:

"But he still maintains his grounds, and still enters court every morning with the same placid air that he would show were he brought there to plead another man's cause and not his own . . . Wilkinson is now before the grand jury and has such a mighty mass of words to deliver himself of that he claims at least two more days to discharge the wondrous cargo [this was June 22]. The first interview between him and Burr was highly interesting, and I secured a good place to witness it. Burr was seated with his back to the entrance, facing the Judge, and conversing with one of his counsel. Wilkinson strutted into court and took his stand in a parallel line with Burr on his right hand. Here he stood for a moment, swelling like a turkeycock, and bracing himself for the encounter of Burr's eye. The latter did not take any notice of him until the Judge directed the clerk to swear General Wilkinson; at the mention of

his name, Burr turned his head, looked him full in the
face with one of his piercing regards, swept his eyes
over his whole person from head to foot, as if to scan
his dimensions, and then coolly resumed his former
position and went on conversing with his counsel tran-
quilly as ever. The whole look was over in an instant;
it was an admirable one . . . . Wilkinson did not
remain in court many minutes.''*

Wilkinson was forced, however, before he was
through with his testimony, to admit that he had altered
parts of the cipher letter; and that he had omitted other
parts which would have incriminated him. Mr. Randolph, as foreman of the jury, called for the letter of
General Wilkinson, which was referred to in the Colonel's cipher letter. But Burr "rose immediately and
declared that no consideration, no calamity, no des-
peration should induce him to betray a letter confiden-
tially written." And this manly attitude struck everyone
in his favor.

John Randolph's comment in a letter to a friend at
that time on the impression that Wilkinson's statement
before the grand jury made upon him, is a valuable
contribution to the vindication of Burr. It reads in
part:

"All was confusion of language and looks. Such a
countenance never did I behold. There was scarcely a
variance of opinion amongst us [the grand jury] as to

*See "Life and Letters of Washington Irving."

his guilt. Yet this miscreant is hugged to the bosom of the government . . . W. is the most finished scoundrel that ever lived; a ream of paper would not contain all the proofs; but what of that? He is the man whom the King delights to honor."

But the grand jury indicted Burr instead of Wilkinson, who later escaped court martial for this perfidy by the small margin of a vote of seven to nine. Even Mr. Hay was convinced of his treachery, and told Mr. Randolph that General Wilkinson was "terrified beyond description" when Daniel Clarke, of New Orleans, appeared at Richmond, saying to Hay that Clarke would ruin him. John Randolph further comments thus on Wilkinson:

"The mammoth of iniquity escaped. Not that any man pretended to think him innocent, but upon certain wiredrawn distinctions . . . W. is the only man that I ever saw, who was from the bark to the core a villain. The proof is unquestionable . . . suffice it to say that I have seen it, and that it is not susceptible to misconstruction. Burr supported himself with great fortitude. . . . Perhaps, you never saw human nature in so degraded a situation as in the person of Wilkinson before the grand jury; and yet this man stands on the very summit and pinnacle of executive favor. . . ."*

General Eaton went strutting about from place to place in a large white hat and Turkish sash making

*Randolph to Nicholson, June 25, 1807.

drunken wagers as to the conviction of Burr, which only added to the reactionary bearing on the case, as had the Wilkinson testimony.

Public opinion was now turning toward the accused. Burr's rooms were thronged with visitors, and he was swamped with flowers, notes of sympathy, and delicacies to eat. Blennerhassett could not comprehend how this "indicted gentleman" should thus enjoy the freedom of Richmond in full view of the United States Marshall, who never did take him into custody. After the indictment, however, Burr spent two nights in jail, as the Chief Justice refused to release him on bond; then he was removed to the home of Luther Martin, where he was placed under guard. But when the trial was deferred until August, he was removed to the State Penitentiary, a mile out of the city, where he was assigned to spacious rooms on the third floor. But let us listen to Burr's own description of the rooms, as given in a letter to his daughter on July 3, 1807:

"I have three rooms in third story of the penitentiary, making an extension to one hundred feet. My jailer is quite a polite and civil man, altogether unlike the idea one would have formed of a jailer . . . My friends and acquaintances of both sexes are permitted to visit me without interruption or question." He is expecting his daughter to come, and he tells her that in case she does arrive that he can give her a bedroom, parlor, and closet—larger than any she has ever had, on this floor.

Then he continues: "Remember, no agitations, no complaints, no fears or anxieties, or I renounce thee." He wanted her to come because he desired to have "an independent and discerning witness to my conduct and to that of the government. The scenes, which have passed, and those that are about to be transacted, will exceed all reasonable credibility, and will hereafter be deemed fables unless attested by very high authority. I repeat what has heretofore been written, that I should never invite anyone, much less those dear to me, to witness my disgrace. I may be inured in dungeons, chained, murdered in legal form, but I cannot be humiliated or disgraced. . . . If absent, you will suffer great solicitude. In my presence, you will feel none, whatever may be the malice or the power of my enemies, and in both they abound." But despite Burr's effort to encourage his daughter in this letter, we catch another glimpse of his life behind these grey, prison walls on July 7 through Washington Irving's letter to Miss Mary Farlie, which has lived through the century and a quarter. Irving had just turned from the prison when he penned this letter. He first comments on the "female goodness" manifested toward Burr in his adversity and then continues:

"They have been uniform in their expressions of compassion for his misfortune and acquittal; not a lady, I believe, in Richmond, whatever may be her husband's sentiment on the subject, who would not rejoice at seeing Colonel Burr at liberty. It may be said that Colonel

Burr has ever been a favorite with the sex; but I am
not inclined to account for it in so ill-liberal a manner;
it results from that merciful and heavenly disposition
implanted in the female bosom which ever inclines in
favor of the accused and the unfortunate. You smile at
the high strain in which I have indulged; believe it is
because I feel it; and I love your sex ten times better
than ever."

Irving further speaks of the prison conditions and the
humiliation of Burr's surroundings in this "abode of
thieves, cut-throats, etc." subject to the deprivations of
a condemned criminal in order to save the state the
cost of properly guarding him. He comments on Burr's
unusual dearth of cheerfulness, and concludes, "I never
felt in a more melancholy mood than when I rode from
that solitary prison. Such is the last interview with poor
Burr, and I shall not forget it. I have written myself into
a sorrowful kind of mood, so I will desist . . ."*

Another interesting witness in this preliminary hearing
at Richmond was Dudley Woodbridge, of Wood
County, Blennerhassett's business partner, and the
builder of the boats for the expedition. Mr. Woodbridge
was confident that Blennerhassett's fortune had been
overestimated; that five or six thousand dollars would
cover the amount that he had in the hands of his agent
at Philadelphia; and that notwithstanding his island
improvement had cost him forty or fifty thousand, he

*Irving's "Life and Letters."

could not sell it for anything like that amount unless it be to a man of his own type. He had about three thousand dollars in stock in their business, and he had given him six thousand for one-half of the profits. Woodbridge admitted that Blennerhassett was a man of literature, but that in the community he stood for having every other kind of sense but common sense. It was also brought out during the examination of Woodbridge that Blennerhassett was so near-sighted that he could not distinguish a man from a horse ten steps away, and that Burr could not possibly have wanted a man of this type for a military enterprise.

Allbright, a laborer on the Island, who testified to the arrest of Blennerhassett by General Tupper on the night of his flight from the Island, was proved to be an unreliable witness, years after when the affidavit of General Tupper was unearthed in Ohio. Allbright's testimony failed in its purpose at the time for the want of a corroborating witness; as he was the only one who testified to the all-essential "overt act," which must be proved in order to bring about a verdict of treason. General Tupper was at Richmond during the trial, but for some unknown reason was not called as a witness.

Israel Miller, who testified that he came to the Island, between December 7-10 with Colonel Tyler and his four boats of thirty-two men, was another interesting

witness, but there was not even a tinge of the overt act
in his story.

> *Note: Testimony of local witnesses, as well as others, is to
> be found in the Burr Trials; but Beveridge in his "Life of John
> Marshall," Volume 3, has interesting comments on them, pages
> 425-27.*

State Penitentiary at Richmond, where Burr was Imprisoned

State Capitol where Trial was Held

9

Trial and Acquittal

The trial, which opened on August 3 was long and excitable. For twenty-six days the battle raged. It involved sixty witnesses and the greatest array of legal talent in the history of the country. Upon the bench sat John Marshall without equal for soundness of judgment and courage, calm, dignified, attentive, and justice-loving, weighing the arguments with the skill of a critic.

"At the bar was Wirt with his soul-stirring eloquence and brilliancy of imagination which swayed the minds of juror and auditor. Martin, who had distinguished himself in the trial of Judge Chase before the United States Senate, was there with his piercing two-edged sword. Hay, everready to take advantage of any suspicious circumstance against the Prisoner, was present in power and might. Randolph, slow, deliberate, and careful; Botts, facetious and playful, but reviewing the whole "scandalous behavior of the government," with fearless clarity; Wickham, dignified and commanding, handling his subject with master hand, were there. And there, too, was Burr, "proudly preeminent in point of intelligence," as defendant in the highest crime against his country. He had the resources and talents of the government arrayed against him, and every faculty of his brilliant mind was called into play in his own defense."

The former high standing of the Defendant and his service to his country; the magnitude of the charge, and the number of persons involved, excited an interest unparalleled in our annals. Richmond was overflowing in spite of the dreadful heat, and the hall was crowded to its capacity all the while.

Blennerhassett was of far less moment—a silent, pathetic figure, preoccupied in some far-a-way mental vision, perhaps that of his ruined home, engaged him day by day as the trial dragged on. But notwithstanding his seeming absorption, his journal proves that he was an attentive listener, and discriminating observer. Second in interest to the Prisoner, was a charming feminine figure, which must ever hold a distinct place in the annals of this famous trial—that of the beautiful Theodosia Burr Alston, "whose love for her father partook of the purity of another world," There is nothing in human history that is more touching. than her devotion during this ordeal. Beautiful, intelligent far beyond the average woman of her time, she was the center of admiration throughout the entire trial. When all the world doubted, she still believed in him, and stood bravely, unswervingly at his side, notwithstanding the stain it must leave on her. She brought with her little Gamp, who was ever a delight to his grandfather, and went about Richmond making valuable friendships by her sweet gentleness of manner.

The two principal witnesses against Burr were the

"perjured Wilkinson," and the "purchased Eaton," both of whom later admitted their infamy. A definite overt act of hostility alone could constitute treason, and according to the ruling of John Marshall "no evidence certainly has any bearing unless the 'overt act' be proved"; and as this proof was wanting, the case could not be sustained. There was nothing introduced to show that Burr had ever planned anything hostile to Spain that was not based upon the event of war between the two countries. Attempts to persuade Blennerhassett to turn state's evidence were all to no avail. The government had no case, and it was in desperate straits after all this ado. Its witnesses nearly all bear the brand of perjury in history today. When the trial ended on September 1 in acquittal, it is said that General Wilkinson "looked like a sergeant under courtmartial"; and Eaton, "more like a fool than ever." The verdict read:

"We of the jury say that Aaron Burr is not proved to be guilty under the indictment by any evidence submitted to us, we, therefore, find him not guilty."

Burr protested against this unusual form of wording, as it seemed equivalent to saying, "We believe in his guilt though it has not been proved to us." Just that interpretation of the verdict has remained in the mind of the public from that day to this. The unfairness of newspaper reports were doubtless largely responsible for many of the wrong impressions that have crept into history and that have supported prejudices and ill-feeling.

Upon receiving the news of the verdict, Theodosia gives us another interesting glimpse behind the scenes in a letter to a close friend:

"I have just this moment received a message from court, announcing to me that the jury brought in a verdict of acquittal, and I hasten to inform you of it, my dear, to allay the anxiety which, with even more of your usual sweetness, you have expressed in your letter of the 22d of July. It afflicts me, indeed, to think that you should have suffered so much from sympathy with the imagined state of my feelings; for the knowledge of my father's innocence, my ineffable contempt for his enemies, and the elevation of his mind have kept me above any sensations bordering on depression. Indeed, my father, so far from accepting of sympathy, has continually animated all around him; it was common for desponding friends, filled with alarm at some occurrence, terrified with some new appearance of danger to fly to him in search of encouragement and support, and be laughed out of their fears by the subject of them. This I have witnessed every day, and it almost persuaded me that he possessed the secret of repelling danger, as well as apprehension of it. Since my residence here, of which some days, and a night, were passed in the penitentiary, our little family circle has been a scene of uninterrupted gaiety. Thus you see, my lovely sister, this visit has been a real party of pleasure. From many of the first inhabitants, I have received the most unremitting and delicate attentions, sympathy, indeed, of any that I have ever experienced."

The trial for misdemeanor followed the acquittal for treason. It seemed to be understood that the purpose of this proceeding was to catch John Marshall, who now stood alongside of Burr in the estimation of the President, and cries of impeachment were in the air. But suffice it to say that this trial, too, ended in acquittal. Five juries —in Kentucky, Tennessee, Mississippi, and Virginia, had now exonerated Burr—what next? exile and persecution. Burr had asked release on bond that he might prove that the finding of the grand jury charge was based on the testimony of perjured witnesses, but this was denied him. After the result of all this investigation, should it not have been sufficient proof that Burr was a wronged man? But alas! it seemed that it was not. Andrew Jackson dubbed the trial "political persecution" and believed Jefferson to be the leader of the cabal, according to Beveridge in the "Life of John Marshall"; and Randolph declared that the "President's declaration of Burr's guilt is (was) unconstitutional." Beveridge says, "Wilkinson, himself, had long contemplated the idea of dismembering the nation, but if Burr ever really considered, as a practical matter, the separation of the Western Country from the Union, his intimate contact with the people of that region had driven such a scheme from his mind and had renewed and strengthened his long cherished wish to invade Mexico." For he had heard loud demands throughout his travels for the expulsion of Spanish rule from America, but never a hint of secession unless at New Orleans. But it did not take these dark rumors long to fly over the route that Burr had travelled with such acclaim, and dim his glory.

The belief that Burr had cleverly inveigled Blennerhassett into his schemes, then impoverished and ruined him, which has been so firmly fixed in the mind of the public for a century and a quarter, is set aside by the brief, which Blennerhassett prepared with his own hand for the Richmond trial, and which is still in existence. He clearly states that he took the initiative in the matter, and his letter in a preceding chapter corroborates this brief.

It is also to Burr's credit, contrary to popular belief, that closely following the trial, Joseph Alston fully settled Blennerhassett's claim entailed by the enterprise by the payment of a sum of twelve thousand five hundred dollars; and some authorities are charitable enough to think that the later demands of Blennerhassett may have been due to an overwrought mind. But let us turn to the journal figures of Blennerhassett concerning this matter:

"I have to-day* spent much time in painful reflection on the state of my affairs with Burr. It appears from a statement of my private account with him, so far as I can now collect all my charges against him here, for

* *This was at the close of the Richmond trial.*

he has two credits, he is indebted to me in a balance of $2,864.96 independent of my account against him for what I have paid and lost by my endorsement of the bill held by Miller for $4,000. It will be useless or worse for me to appear at Marietta without a sum of money, if not sufficient to discharge Miller's claim, at least necessary to enable me to get my negroes away from Ohio, if that is now possible, and to redeem some few articles of my property that have been sacrificed at sheriff's sales.''

The aggregate sum then of Burr's obligation to Blennerhassett at the close of the Richmond trial was $6,864.96. Alston's check amounted to almost twice that sum, though Blennerhassett evidently experienced difficulty in getting it. His later demand, however, was for $50,000 with the Alston check credited. Though an innovation here, let us see what Mrs. Alston has to say in verification of this debt having been cancelled in a letter to her father from the Oaks on May 10, 1811, when the contention arose again:

"Would you believe it, Blennerhassett has written the most insulting letter to my husband. In this letter, he accuses you and him of plans which never entered the head of either of you; and says that unless Mr. Alston pays him $35,000 of which to use his own phrase, he demands fifteen thousand by August; unless these sums are paid, he (Blennerhassett) will publish a pamphlet containing documents which must ruin him (Mr.

Alston) forever. He concludes by saying that his work
is all ready for publication, and adds:

"If you do not prevent its appearance, you may rest
assured I shall not, to save the trouble of smelting,
abandon the ore I have with such expense and labor
exhausted from the mines both dark and deep, not
indeed of Mexico, but of Alston, Jefferson, and Burr.
Having mentioned Mr. Burr, I wish to observe that I
have long since ceased to consider reference to his honor,
resources, or good faith in any other light than as scandal
to any man offering it, who is not sunk as low as
himself, etc.

"His language to Mr. Alston is the same style. Such,
in short, as a low-bred coward may use at the distance
of many hundred miles. Did you ever hear of such an
audacious, swindling trick? Mr. Alston has not deigned
to answer him. Thus we are to have a new scene which
will make a great noise, and end in confusion for the
author. The debt you contracted is paid." Thus Mrs.
Alston unwittingly verifies the fact that Mr. Alston
has paid the debt, and betrays her astonishment at the
demand.

Returning to the court proceedings, Blennerhassett
was never tried. On Monday, September 1, 1807, the
day of Burr's acquittal, we find this notation in his
journal:

"This day at 11 o'clock a. m. ended my captivity,
which lasted fifty-three days. I was taken down to

court about 10 o'clock when Mr. Botts called upon Mr. Hay to know what he meant to do with my treason bill, which Hay agreed to have discharged, but required my detension on the indictment for misdemeanor, which produced a conversation on the subject of bail, during which Woodbridge [of Wood County] was accepted as surety." Thus Blennerhassett was released, and was never again molested on any of the remaining charges; for Burr was acquitted of the misdemeanor and this concluded the detention at Richmond.

Blennerhassett's comments in his journal during the trial are very interesting glimpses. On one occasion he notes his impressions of Wirt thus:

"Wirt spoke very much to engage the fancy of his hearers to-day, without affecting their understanding; for he cannot reason upon the subject before him, and can no more conduct a law argument than I could raise a mountain. As Junius says of the King, 'The feather that adorns him supports his flight. Strip him of his plumage and you fix him to the earth.' He attempted to be sarcastic to all his opponents."

10

From Richmond to Natchez

Now let us follow Blennerhassett through the pages of his journal from Richmond until he joins his family at Natchez in February. It is October 28, 1807 when he reaches Washington City, which is still in its swaddling clothes, and this is his impression of the youngster:

"This city has certainly no resemblance to any other on earth. Its extent as originally laid out has been known for some years past upon paper, but a few singular features, as they now smile and frown upon the Potomac, are remarkable. As to streets, literally speaking, there is not one yet in existence unless the few wide paths and half-made roads that intersect each other can be called streets. On a hill at the head of one of these about a mile from the river stand the two wings, without body, of what constitute, but is already called, the Capitol. These are cumbrous, ill-proportioned piles of building to my eye, with too small space for the central building, if ever reared. About another mile's distance to the westward stands the President's House, with a low, dead-wall front, and an ordinary post and rail fence in the rear of it. On either side of it stand what are called its wings, which any person would require to be told were such before he could believe it; for they are brick and at too great a distance to appear to belong to the large white house between them any more than to the Capitol. They are each in a row of ordinary brick houses; in those to the west is kept the post-office; in those to the east, the Secretary of State's office, etc.; and both, it is said, are to be connected with the center of the garden. But the last feature of architecture has not yet made its appearance. From the Capitol you behold in four or five directions at the distance of from one to four miles apart, rows of houses each of five or six together, so that the whole appears like a jumble of fragments of villages, except that part being one and a half miles northeast of the Capitol where the navy yard is said to stand, which is more built up than any other quarter of the city. But after all, every foreigner after his arrival here will inquire for fifty years to come, as is now very common, 'where is the city of Washington?' "

Blennerhassett left Washington on October 30, for Baltimore, where he and Burr, Luther Martin and others narrowly escaped mob violence. Plans for the execution in effigy of John Marshall and the three above named, had been laid, and handbills in satirical language lay all about the city. Martin demanded protection of the mayor by law, and the police were sent to the Evans hotel where Blennerhassett was registered. Acting upon advice, he concealed himself in the attic of the hotel where he watched the proceedings from the window; as he had been informed that the mob meant to tar and feather him. Martin's law students protected him; Burr and Swartwout were escorted to the stage-coach office by guards and left hastily for Philadelphia. John Marshall was not present, but it seems that the hanging in effigy did take place, amidst the clamor.

Leaving Baltimore, Blennerhassett continued his journey by way of Philadelphia to Marietta, where he arrived on December 15 for the purpose of answering the misdemeanor charge in Ohio, but it was never called. He visited the Island and sadly viewed its desolation.

The mansion and grounds bore no semblance to the paradise that he had left behind a little more than a year before. The destructive hand of the militia had been aided by neglect, floods, and freebooters, until the fair gardens and lawns were a sorry sight. Everything portable had been carried away. The library and remaining furniture had been sold at cruel sacrifice, and the Island, itself, had been extended by writ of eligit to Robert Miller of Kentucky, who had already begun the culture of hemp and the manufacture of cordage on it. Friends of his prosperity were friends no more; creditors were harsh and insulting; and Blennerhassett turned away with heavy heart and continued his journey back to his little family at Natchez, arriving in February.

Burr remained incognito as much as possible after the trial until the following June when he slipped away to Europe.

11

The Shadows Deepen into Night

After his return to Natchez, Blennerhassett purchased a thousand acres, six miles from Gibson Port, on the Mississippi, and set about retrieving his fortune. Cotton now commanded exorbitant prices and he installed a cotton-gin. With the slaves and the help of Mrs. Blennerhassett, who mounted her horse and carried instructions to the overseer each morning, Prosperity once again began to smile.

But the war of 1812 came on; the market went to pieces, and the promising outlook faded from sight. In the meantime, during the summer of 1811, the mansion on the Island was accidentally destroyed by fire, which lent another blow to expectations from that direction. Then on November 6, 1816, we find Harman Blennerhassett and his wife, Margaret, of Claiborne County, Mississippi, selling the beloved Island to Joseph L. Lewis, of Philadelphia for the inadequate sum of ten thousand dollars, paid in hand or before the "sealing of this deed." In this grant Blennerhassett describes this tract "as that part of land situated on the first Island in the river Ohio below the mouth of the Little Kanawha in the county of Wood, and in the state of Virginia, containing by estimate two hundred acres more or less; and is that tract of land deeded by the high court of chancery holden at Staunton, Virginia in said state, to be conveyed by Elijah Backus to the said Harman Blennerhassett, and is usually known and designated by the appellation of Blennerhassett Island."* All appurtenances, privileges, and advantages were transferred to Mr. Lewis by this transaction, which was recorded on May 14, 1817. But Robert Miller, who had been in possession since 1807, under writ of eligit, entered suit for damages and was granted two judgments one of $4,000, and the other of $360, which had to be satisfied out of the transaction.

However, we leave Joseph L. Lewis of Philadelphia, in charge of the precious Island, and return to the Mississippi plantation, "La Cache" where the Blennerhassetts remained for twelve years, whatever may have been the status of their success, which is asserted by one and contradicted by another. They then sold this home for $28,000 and went to Canada, 1819, after an extended visit with the Emmetts in New York, while enroute. They settled at Montreal where Blennerhassett formed a law partnership with an old school friend, and remained at the bar until 1822, when he decided to return to the homeland in the interest of an estate, which he was to learn no longer existed.

What must have been his feelings as the land faded from sight, and the vast deep spread out before him,

---

* See deed book 5, p. 305, Wood County records. Also later chapter Continuous Ownership of the Island.

leaving him alone with his reflections! Strange circumstances had attended his every footstep for the past
quarter of a century in this new world. It was Youth
with adventurous spirit that had come to these shores.
It was now a disappointed man of middle life that was
returning to the land of his birth to claim its bounty
and to plead for its attention in his reverses. The dreams
of youth had vanished; the hopes of maturer years had
found an early tomb; the quiet and seclusion sought had
been turned into conflict and pitiless publicity. This
man had lived to see every prospect blighted, every
plan, defeated.

The future must have looked vague and shadowy with
apprehension as his feet once again touched native soil.
Unlike the Prodigal, there was no fond father's embrace,
no best robe, no fatted calf; for the friends of his youth
were no more. Blennerhassett was practically a stranger
in his own native land. The heritage he sought was
debarred by limitation; the judgeship had been claimed
by another. Heavy-hearted he wandered from place to
place hoping against hope, while the separation from
his wife, who was having almost unbearable hardships
in trying to care for her children, added poignantly to
his grief. It has been said that his sister came to his
rescue at once by willing her property to him, but this
is questionable in the face of the fact that he remained
three years before his return, and Mrs. Blennerhassett's

letters,* which disclose her struggles for maintenance during his prolonged stay.

Soon after his departure, she took her two sons, Harman and Joseph Lewis, and went to her sister's, Mrs. Dow, at Wilkesbarre, Pennsylvania, where she remained until December, following. Separation from her husband and eldest son, Dominick, who was seeking employment in the South, almost overwhelmed her with grief, at times. Her letters to her husband are filled with pathos and loyalty. Never once does she reproach him for the hardships that have come upon her, but it is through their undertone of despair that one catches the best glimpse of the worthlessness and intemperance of Dominick, and the cruel disappointment that it brought to her fond mother-heart. But this trial turned to one of sorrow and apprehension when he dropped from sight, 1823, and was never heard of again. On June 27, 1824, she wrote to her husband that she had heard nothing from him for a year. His fate was never known.

It was not far from this period that she published her book, "The Widow on the Rock and Other Poems." She was then at Montreal and was in such straitened circumstances that she was compelled to call upon the Emmetts for financial aid for the necessities of life. Her book failed to bring the hoped-for return. In her

* See what Blennerhassett Papers tell in later chapter.

despair, at times, she wondered "what I have done to merit such sorrow?"

She wrote to her husband on one occasion, "All these little attentions paid me at first by many of the citizens of this community seemed to have been withdrawn until the publication of my book, which in a few instances excited renewal of them, and which I have rejected; holding it better to live in solitude than again subject myself to the capriciousness of those to whom I feel myself superior. The Author of the 'Widow on the Rock and other Poems' will, therefore, receive no favor, which has been withheld from Mrs. Blennerhassett."

In 1825, after three years of painful separation and apparently fruitless wanderings, Blennerhassett returned to Canada, and with his wife and youngest son, sailed from Quebec never to return. His maiden sister, Avice Blennerhassett, had offered him a home with her for the rest of his life (or willed him her estate as some aver). They lived at Cottage Crescent, Bath, for a while; then for the benefit of Mrs. Blennerhassett's health, removed to the milder climate of Jersey Island, in the English Channel, and finally to the landed property of Avice Blennerhassett in the Isle of Guernsey. Here, weary with the buffetings of a cold world, Harman Blennerhassett fell asleep at 2 o'clock on the morning of February 2, 1831, just a few hours after suffering a second stroke of paralysis. The wife whose loyalty and devotion had stood the test of unprecedented trials for thirty-five years, administered to his last needs. Joseph Lewis Blennerhassett, then nineteen, was called from college, and he and his mother erected a monument over his grave, which bears the following unique inscription:

> "*Here lies Harman Blennerhassett, Esq., LL.B.*
> *Barrister of Law of the Kings Inns, Dublin.*
> *He passed through a variety of changes during his active life. Nearly thirty years of which he passed in the U. S. A. & Canada. While in America at one time he owned a most beautiful Island in the Ohio River which still bears his name. He was a man of (. . .) true piety to his Creator, philanthropy and virtue, and was possessed of great acquired and natural ability and talents. He departed this life on the 2nd of February A. D. 1831 in the 63d year of his age. His bereaved wife and son caused this monument to be erected to his memory . . ."*
> *Strangers pass not by without dropping a tear."*

Mrs. Blennerhassett remained in England until 1840, when she returned to New York to the bedside of her son, Harman, who was then an invalid, and for the purpose of imploring Congress to aid her in securing redress for the wanton destruction of her Island home in the Ohio. The Memorial was presented to Congress and found ardent champions in Henry Clay and Robert Addis Emmett, who emphasized her great needs and the justice of the cause. But while Congress dallied, the dark-winged messenger of Death intervened, and Margaret Agnew Blennerhassett passed beyond all need of earthly help on June 16, 1842, after a few hours illness at her rented home, at 75 Greenwich Street, New York.

She was just on the eve of returning to England to live with her sisters.

The oft repeated story of her dying alone with no one near, is wholly without foundation. Joseph Lewis, the youngest son, who was then married and living at Swansea, South Wales, had come on to New York for the purpose of lending his aid to his mother in the bill that was pending in Congress, and she died in his arms. Harman was also present. She was the idol of these sons, who followed her to the grave. She and Mrs. Thomas Addis Emmett were devoted friends, and years before they had expressed the wish that they might lie in the same grave. In accord with this wish, their caskets rest side by side in the Emmett family vault in St. Paul's at Broadway.*

Congress never took action on the Memorial, neither does it seem that absolute need demanded it, though justice surely did. But the heirs never gave up hope of recovering the Island. Thirty-nine years after the flight of Blennerhassett on that dark, December night, we

*Owing to changes and confusion in the Emmet Family Vaults in New York, the location of this cemetery cannot be verified to-day. But as Harman Blennerhassett II rests in the T. A. Emmet Vault in the Second Street Marble Cemetery, this is doubtless where his mother rests. Mrs. Emmet survived Mrs. Blennerhassett by four years.

Later: We have been able at last to verify by a reliable eye witness, who read the inscriptions on the vaults of Margaret Blennerhassett and Mrs. Emmett, years ago, that they do both rest in this cemetery.

find his son, Harman, engaged in correspondence with an attorney over the possibility of recovering it for the heirs under the laws of Virginia, but this hope was never realized. There is no evidence, however, to substantiate the story that Mrs. Blennerhassett had to support the children after his death. She had but two living, and they had reached manhood's estate, and but one was on that side of the Atlantic.

12

The Blennerhassett Descendants

The Blennerhassett family is now extinct. The blight that touched the parent tree withered its fair blossoms. The two little daughters died in childhood. Dominick, the eldest son, though well educated, seemed to be a worthless, drunken sot. He disappeared at St. Louis in 1823, and the Mississippi is supposed to hold the secret of his fate.

Harman Blennerhassett II, a lawyer, died in New York City, 1854, after a long invalidism. He was without doubt shiftless and intemperate, but his letters late in life do not bear out the statement that he was "half-witted" as some writers avow. Neither was he dependent upon charity, though it seems that the class of his associates in his intemperance, left this impression. There is no mention of his marriage but he left no heirs.

Joseph Lewis, the youngest son, who was born on the plantation in Mississippi, is said to have been of the intemperate persuasion, too, though he was well-educated in Europe and was an attorney at Troy, Missouri, during the latter part of his life. His letters, which are on file in the Library of Congress up to 1863, not far from the time of his death, are in beautiful hand, and otherwise bespeak a high degree of education and intelligence. He was evidently married twice, as Therese

Blennerhassett says that he was married and living at
Swansea, South Wales in 1840, and he did not return
to the United States until 1847 to make his home. Then
in 1859, we find him writing to this same cousin
Therese Blennerhassett as follows:

"Joseph Lewis Blennerhassett lately married a widow
lady, and now has a beautiful son named Robert Emmett Blennerhassett, who up to this period may be
called 'The last of the Island Family'—Third after
Mrs. Blennerhassett's return from Europe to the United
States." Joseph Lewis Blennerhassett had another son,
Harman III, but death claimed both of these sons, before
it did the father, and this ends the line of the Island
Blennerhassetts—the sad, sad story of a tragedy that
would be hard to duplicate in human history. The date
of the death of Joseph Lewis Blennerhassett is given
December 8, 1862, but this is incorrect, since his correspondence does not cease until during the winter of
1863.

On August 4, 1863, Mrs. Alice Blennerhassett, of
St. Louis, in writing to J. Delbert Tyndall, speaks of
the "death of our mutual friend Mr. Blennerhassett,"
and inquires about some jewelry and other articles,
which evidently belonged to the family. Tyndall, in
replying, says, that the only thing that Mr. Blennerhassett left to him was the "Memoirs of his late Father
in connection with Vice President Burr, which book
he presented to me in his own handwriting" [the Safford

Publication]. This seems to accurately fix the date of the death of Joseph Lewis Blennerhassett between the months of February, the date of his last letter on file, and August, 1863. His notary public certificate is also on file among the other papers.

In some dissatisfaction over the royalty of the Safford book, we find Mrs. T. M. Blennerhassett, April 1866, in correspondence with Thomas Addis Emmett, of New York, seeking legal advice in regard to bringing suit against Safford. Again in October of the same year, Mr. Emmett "sees nothing to do about it."

13

What the Blennerhassett Papers Tell

The Blennerhassett Papers, which cover the period from 1755-1866, are wonderfully preserved in the manuscript division of the Library of Congress where they were deposited by Therese Blennerhassett Adams in 1921. They include six large volumes classified as to years; Blennerhassett's journals which cover the Richmond trial and the flight from the Island, as well as other periods of his life. His certificate of admission to the Kings Inn, 1790; his certificate of graduation from this institution under date of November 18, 1795; bank checks which show his business relations on both sides of the water; his long drawn-out letter to his nephew, Tom de Courcey, upon his landing in New York; the printed report of the findings of the grand jury in Kentucky on December 5, 1806 with its summary dismissal of Burr after the examination of seventeen witnesses, with the attendant assurance that "there is no grounds for the rumors against Colonel Burr"; voluminous correspondence between Mr. and Mrs. Blennerhassett during enforced and painful separation, and their correspondence with members of the family, attorneys, etc.; and Blennerhassett's brief as prepared by his own hand for the Richmond trial which throws much light on the tragic story and sets aside many a foundationless rumor which has been given credence for a century.

But the object of this review is merely to touch interesting sidelights, which are not included in the general story, for the preceding chapters are based upon these papers and other record accounts.

As we turned the pages of these closely penned manuscripts with an eager expectancy which must have been akin to that of the archaeologist who dives into the ruins of the past, we came upon this amusing circular:

"AWFUL!!

"The public are hereby notified that four choice spirits are this afternoon at three o'clock to be marshalled for execution by the hangman on 'Gallows Hill' in consequence of the sentence pronounced against them by unanimous voice of every honest man in the community. Their respective crimes for which they suffer are thus stated on the record:

"Chief Justice M. . . . (1) for his tricks which are said to be much aggravated by his felonious capers in court on the plea of 'irrevalancy'; (2) His Quid Majesty charged with the trifling fault of wishing to divide the Union and form Bastrop's grant . . .; (3) Blennerhassett, the chemist, convicted of conspiring to destroy the tone of the public fiddle; (4) and last but not least in crime, Lawyer Brandy Bottle for a false, scandalous prophesy that before six months Aaron Burr would divide the Union."

"N. B.—The execution of accomplices is postponed to a future day."

This is a copy of the circulars which were thrown about the streets at Baltimore when Blennerhassett, Burr, and others narrowly escaped mob violence as related in an earlier chapter; but Marshall was not at Baltimore.

Volume III contains a well-written article of sixteen pages, which, though without signature, is unmistakably in the hand of Joseph Lewis Blennerhassett. It reads in part:

"(a) Blennerhassett

"This short but literally true narrative states in general terms most of the principal features of the history of the gentleman and his family who became a citizen of the United States, owned an island in the Ohio river which still bears his name, and who in connection with the late Colonel Aaron Burr obtained a rather singular notoriety among the editorial gentry of America.

"The reader will not think in the least that these facts have been studiously written out to refute personal attacks on the private character, as they certainly are so to aid the literary blockheads of the notorious American press in the correctness of these gratuitous discoveries of the hidden mysteries set forth to edify the *whole nation* without the least shadow of facts or the least deference to the feelings of the connection of the persons they libelously drag into their scurrilous scribblings; and who for the sake of a little literary capital demean themselves and the great national press of which they are unworthy members."

Then the story of the family of Blennerhassett follows, with the omission of the names of several of his sisters, which hides a number of important facts, and confirms others. Such as their never having been in want; the time of their leaving Mississippi and spending the interval with the Emmetts in New York, while en route to Canada. This article also testifies to Blennerhassett's being the beneficiary of his sister, Avice's will, and to the inscription on his monument.

But correspondences over the affairs following the death of Avice Blennerhassett in 1838, do not bear out the statement of her wholesale "gift of deed" of her property to her brother, though there is no doubt that she shared her bounty with the family and left something to Mrs. Blennerhassett at her death. The stories of want are ever denied by the family and by some historians; but let us listen to the plaintive tones of Mrs. Blennerhassett—in extracts from her letters, during his three years of absence and fruitless wanderings in Europe: In her great disappointment on one occasion she says: "Though I had no idea that fortune would ever smile upon us again, at least to any great extent," implies that she had not expected it to be so bad. Her tone of distress runs through all of her letters, as does her unwavering devotion. Never once does she reproach her husband because of her suffering, but always seems to encourage him, bravely bearing her part.

Her greatest trial at this time seemed to be the intemperance and utter irresponsibility of Dominick, who was ever reappearing when she thought he had work, and who was a constant care. In one of her letters, she tells her husband of the return of his old habits and of his homecoming for her to support, and adds: "The most hopeless idiot has no more claim on a mother's care than he, for I firmly believe he has no longer power to refrain from drink. I had no money, having for some weeks paid by borrowing from Mr. Emmett, because having looked for you by the spring ships, I wished not to encumber the Montreal Bank Stock."

Later in speaking of Dominick she opens her breaking heart thus: "Harman sought him out and found him already enlisted [in the army] and brought him to me at the steamboat hotel, dressed in a common soldier's garb but quite happy and unconcerned. O God! had I been guilty of the greatest crime, the punishment of that moment ought to have expatiated it! but the subject is too painful to dwell upon. I will only add that he went with the detachment up the Mississippi and is now I believe, acting as surgeon's mate, and as yet I have received no communication from him." This may have been the last time she saw him before he disappeared forever.

Joseph Lewis Blennerhassett in a letter to his cousin, Therese Blennerhassett, on July 15, 1859 gives the following description of his mother:

"Margaret Blennerhassett, my mother, was not musical. It was the only fault my father ever found with her—that she had not so 'fine an ear for music' as he had. Poetry was her bent. British Continental, moral philosophy, history, and literature, she loved. Her conversational talent was of the highest order, . . . her information for a female was immense and impressively correct, and this combined with her beauty of person and feature . . . with inexhaustible sallies of wit, caused her society to be always courted. She was exceedingly pious, gentle, and humane; the best of wives, the best of mothers—in fact heir to every female and domestic virtue." He then verifies the birth of the children as given in a former chapter.

The following letter, which was written in one of the darkest hours of her life, will serve as a criterion of her loyalty and self-effacement throughout: It was written from Natchez, August 3, 1807—

"My dearest Love:—After having experienced the greatest disappointment in not hearing from you for two mails, I, at length, heard of your arrest. I think that had you of your own accord, gone to Richmond and solicited a trial, it would have accorded better with your pride, and you would have escaped the unhappiness of missing my letters which every week I wrote to Marietta. God knows what you may feel or suffer on our account before this reaches you, to inform you of our health and welfare in every particular; and knowing this, I trust and feel your mind will rise superior to every inconvenience that your present situation may subject you to. Let no solicitude, whatever, for us, damp your spirits. We have many friends here, who do the utmost in their power to counteract any disagreeable sensation occasioned by your absence. I shall live in the hope of hearing from you by the next mail; and entreat you, by all that is dear to us, not to let any disagreeable feelings on account of our separation enervate your mind at this time. Remember that all here will read with great interest anything concerning you; but still do not trust too much to yourself; consider your want of practice at the bar, and spare not the fee of a lawyer. Apprise Colonel Burr of my warmest acknowledgments for his own and Mrs. Alston's kind remembrance; and tell him to assure her she has inspired me with a warmth of attachment which can never diminish. I wish him to urge her to write to me.

"God bless you—prays your   —M. Blennerhassett."

After Burr's return from Europe, Blennerhassett renewed his demand for reimbursement to the amount of fifty thousand dollars, with the acknowledgment of the twelve thousand five hundred already paid by Alston, deducted; and reiterated his threats to issue the publication, exposing the scheme which had fallen into his hands, under the title of "A Review of the Projects and Intrigues of Aaron Burr During the Years 1805-7." These threats were based upon documents that fell into Blennerhassett's hands unwittingly, and it seems that Burr could not have been aware that they were in his possession until he thus explains in a letter of October 4, 1812:

"As to the manner in which I obtained the papers, it happened to be disclosed that the portmanteau you left with me to be transmitted to Mr. Alston, which lay at my disposal in the house of Mr. Harding, near Natchez, was broken open by the servants. On this discovery, I called for the portmanteau, found the back torn off and some papers tumbled and abused, which had seemingly all been opened. In folding and tying them up I observed and took out the above document. The rest together with silk tent await the disposition of your order."

This letter with Burr's other papers was turned over to M. L. Davis, his authorized biographer, at his death, and through the correspondence of Davis and Mrs. Blennerhassett its contents are now among the Blennerhassett papers in the form of Davis's letter.

Mrs. Blennerhassett held these papers in her possession and at the death of Colonel Burr, she hastened to advertise them for the benefit of his biographers. Among other things she says:

"In consequence of the recent death of Colonel Burr whose eventful life will no doubt be published, I lose no time in advertizing to his biographers that I am in possession of the most ample document for removing mystery which has hitherto enveloped those events which agitated the United States in 1806-7.

"These documents were carefully preserved by my late husband, Harman Blennerhassett, and since his death, as carefully preserved by me with a view to their future publication, the time for which has now arrived; it only remains for me to state my terms which shall bring them to light or consign them to *oblivion* . . . They implicate some of the most conspicuous characters in the Union in what was termed a conspiracy, how far it merits that appellation the public will best judge when the original letters of Colonel Burr and others concerned with him, together with the extension notes of Mr. Blennerhassett (which notes will form an extra volume at least) are published." She concludes by offering the document for adequate remuneration or "I will publish them together with full statement of all circumstances that fell under my observation." In her correspondence with Davis, she refers him to her son, Harman, in New York for terms. Recent writers observe that "Blennerhassett was always boiling with revelations but nothing came of it."

But among these papers is another letter, clearly in the hand of Harman Blennerhassett II, though without signature, which throws light on this matter, and leaves one to strongly suspect that Mrs. Blennerhassett got her price for this document, and that it met its Waterloo in the hands of Davis, who has been charged with incorrectness of fact in his biography of Burr by more than one authority.

This letter, however, is prefaced with a protest concerning the unfairness and inaccuracy of the Davis Memoirs of Burr; and states that he sought documents of Mrs. Blennerhassett in reference to her husband's former connection with Burr for this purpose; that she sent the papers to Davis, and that "little was used." So in the light of the fact that this particular document was the one involved in the correspondence between Mrs. Blennerhassett and Davis, and this protest over the little that she sent being used, one is justified in surmising the fate of that document which was so replete with "revelations."

This letter also verifies the story already given of Burr's first visit to the Island, and sums up Blennerhassett's deliberations on the Burr project thus:

"The latter [Blennerhassett] with good reason concluded that the great talents of Burr would be of service to him, although very large sums of money had been consumed on the improvement and purchase of the Island and the importation of goods for the business affairs of D. Woodbridge & Company, about that time. Blennerhassett (from his great hospitality) found himself somewhat in debt. The Island was too small for his immediate agricultural wants. He had the prospect of a growing family and from the extreme dullness of everything in Ohio and Virginia at that time—the terrible barriers of the Alleghenies, excluding facilities of business from the Atlantic states; and the length and dangers of river navigation yet to surmount in the attaining of a Southern market caused him to contemplate somewhat a visit of speculation in the more southwestern part and possibly New Orleans."

While accusing Burr of warily ensnaring Blennerhassett into this scheme by "making insidious advances to his confidence in the garb of friendship," this letter really contributes much to the vindication of Burr and to his justification in refusing further payment to Blennerhassett, who took matters into his own hands in seeking this step outside of the obligation, which had already been cancelled by Alston.

Another interesting paragraph is the close up view of the beautiful Theodosia Burr Alston, which reads:

"Of that remarkable ill-fated lady, I shall merely remark that she was devoted to her father whom she deified; and in turn for the great attention shown to him and her by the Blennerhassetts, her grateful acknowledgment inwardly seemed endless. She had received entire what is called a French education with a classical one . . . Could fence and shoot off pistols with great precision. Like her father, her person was small, while to its enchanting symmetry and expression of countenance, illuminated by vast reading, her imposing mein and flashing wit made her the ruling spirit of any circle."

Another interesting disclosure of this letter is that of the identity of Colonel Tyler, who figured so conspicuously in the Burr affair. Tyler was a native of Schenectady, New York—a lawyer engaged in chancery, and thirty thousand dollars which had come into his hands from his friends had disappeared along with him, and his whereabouts were unknown until he bobbed up in this Burr affair. A comment is also made on General Washington's distrust of General Wilkinson during the Revolution, and of his being under the surveillance of General Wayne.

It is interesting to observe the prejudices of Harman Blennerhassett II, though, aside from his bias of opinion, he seems absolutely truthful in his statements, while Joseph Lewis Blennerhassett more often leaves the impression of talking for effect.

It was Harman II that furnished the information for the famous Wallace denunciatory article on Burr in the "American Review" back in the fifties of the past century, which appears in part in the chapter entitled "Comments on Burr" in this volume. Through this tirade we catch a bit of the bitterness of Harman II—a bitterness that did not seem to exist in his parents for

Burr, especially in his mother. He not only furnished Wallace the material for this article, but remarked later when asked for information concerning this Burr affair that that "American Review story" was the only authentic story that had ever appeared or ever would appear; for he had refused to give the papers over to the public. But Joseph Lewis Blennerhassett saw things differently and he made terms of publication with Safford, after the death of Harman II. Then Fate decreed that stories over which he held no power were yet to come—that the hidden was to be brought to light; the mystery, revealed.

14

Affidavit of Young Adventurers

From an affidavit made, for Mrs. Blennerhassett in her appeal to Congress for redress, by Morgan Neville and William Robinson, junior, jointly, we get the following first-hand picture of the riotous scene on the Island when the Militia took charge of it upon the flight of Blennerhassett:

Their boat was driven ashore by wind about one mile below the Blennerhassett Mansion as they descended the river, on December 13, 1806, and suddenly they were attacked by a well-armed mob of twenty-five men, who detained them and took them to the mansion, while their boat was surrounded by a guard. When they arrived at the Blennerhassett home, it was filled with militia. Another party of this militia was making fires of rails from the fences that surrounded the home. They demanded services of the servants and when refused, the negroes were harshly driven to the washhouse in fright. These young men were detained from Saturday until Tuesday morning, and during all that time, there were never fewer than thirty men, sometimes from seventy to eighty living in riot on the provisions of Mrs. Blennerhassett. When they left the Island, the cornfields were full of cattle, it seems that corn un-gathered still remained in the field nearest the house; as the fences had been pulled down to keep the fires burning, and destruction from drunken and lawless hands was everywhere present both within and without the beautiful mansion, when these young men left.

15

The Mystery Revealed—a Sequel

Whispers of some dark mystery in the lives of the Blennerhassetts has ever hung mist-like about their names and the ill-fated island. The idea of persons of their bearing and wealth seeking seclusion in this wilderness for such a castle was too much for Madame Grundy, who fostered all sorts of suspicions and gossip; but Fate in her decrees knew how to guard well her secrets, and the Blennerhassetts had long been sleeping when the mystery was revealed—in fact their descendants had all passed from hearing before the veil was removed. It awaited Therese Blennerhassett Adams, a member of a collateral branch of the family to clear up the mystery in her "True Story of Harman Blennerhassett" in Century Magazine, 1901; and her story is verified in Foster's "Noble and Gentle Families of Royal Descent."

Mrs. Therese Blennerhassett Adams was in some way connected with the publication of the Safford book, 1859, which included the Blennerhassett Papers, and during her correspondence with Joseph Lewis Blennerhassett, who furnished her with additional information concerning the family, she evidently mentioned this mystery to him; as she had seen the story of this scandal in a New York paper, accredited to the "Richmond

Whig." But he vehemently denied any knowledge of it, asserted that no one could prove it, if it were true, and insisted that "It is our duty to ourselves and to those who come after to deny the alligations, and to dare these slanderers in the dark to prove it." She had evidently intimated that it came from the Blennerhassett family, and he thinks this impossible.

But in support of this, we find among these letters one from R. Wheatley, of Louisville, Kentucky, an attorney for the Blennerhassetts, who, in trying to settle up the estate, 1843, wrote to a Blennerhassett at St. Louis, thinking it might possibly be the missing Dominick. This letter brought a response from R. J. Blennerhassett, whose father claimed to be the only rightful heir of Harman Blennerhassett, and he dropped a hint concerning the legality of the marriage, which mystified the attorney; for he was just about to bring suit for the recovery of some property for the two sons, and demanded an explanation as to this new claimant to heritage. The explanation was evidently long delayed, but finally came, and Wheatley in his reply, says in part:

"The fact that you mention in regard to the marriage of Harman Blennerhassett . . . enables me to account for circumstances in the conduct of Mrs. Blennerhassett, which before was a mystery to me." He then says that he has already instituted suit in behalf of the two sons for real estate, "which in justice to them they are entitled to recover at all events," and advises silence in regard to the marriage lest the entanglement of an affidavit and a visit to Ireland for additional proof should enter in. He later receives the assurance from this same R. J. Blennerhassett that his "father will not contest the rights of the sons."

Mrs. Adams's story is in substance as follows:

The Blennerhassett Family was a wealthy and prominent one in Ireland. Harman had a number of sisters, who had carried this wealth into titled circles. One was the wife of Lord Kingsale, the premier baron of Ireland; another was married to his brother, the Honorable Michael de Courcey, admiral of the Blue; the wife of Daniel McGilly Cudy, the high sheriff of Kerry; and the wife of Captain Coxon, were others; Avice Blennerhassett remained single and came to his rescue with her fortune in his extremity; and Katherine was the wife of Captain Robert Agnew, the lieutenant governor of the Isle of Man, and the mother of Margaret Blennerhassett.

It was just at the close of his law course, as we already know, that he took a tour of the Continent and visited his sister on the Isle of Man. He was now a man of thirty-one and Margaret Agnew, then a girl of eighteen, was away at school, and he was sent to accompany her home. The distance between Ireland and England was not bridged for rapid travel as it is now, and it is safe to conjecture that he had not seen his niece since her childhood, if he had seen her at all. However, when he met her, he was so completely disarmed by her charm and grace, that he seemed to forget his mission as protector, and all else under the spell of the moment, and in crossing the English Channel, he persuaded her to marry him. But when they returned to her parental home, and he presented his bride, in the consternation and events that quickly followed, there came an awakening that turned the whole course of his life. Greeting turned to scorn for such a breach of honor and law. Blennerhassett being of mature years was held responsible, but Margaret Agnew Blennerhassett was turned from her parental home and disinherited, just when she needed love and protection in her youthful folly. To remain in England or Ireland either meant social ostracism, and Harman Blennerhassett, with his beautiful girl-bride, fled to the wilds of Young America, but this guilty secret haunted him to life's last hour.

It was this secret that laid the foundation for the magic castle in the midst of the fair Ohio; it was this haunting fear—lest his children might learn the truth, as civilization drew nearer, that prompted his rash act in joining the Burr expedition; as he wished to withdraw farther into the wilderness, for he knew that there were persons on this side of the water already that were in possession of his secret. And the Island was now a center of interest for the great who traveled this river. So the unveiling of this mystery sets aside many a foundationless story, which has been woven about this Island and the Builder of the mansion. For nothing else brought the Blennerhassetts here, but this unfortunate romance. Their families would not countenance the marriage, and society would not accept it. This revelation, alongside of court records and Blennerhassett's own brief, exonerating Burr from intriguing him into this entanglement, goes far toward reversing the many stories that have gone before and that have helped to sustain prejudice for a century.

Mrs. Adams insists that though the Blennerhassetts had financial reverses at different times, largely due to their own extravagance and mismanagement, they were never in want; that his people with their means would not have seen them in need, even though they could not tolerate the marriage; and that her sisters always laid aside a part of their share and sent it to her. She also says that Harman II, in his intemperance, associated with the sort of people that gave rise to the poverty story, but that he was never an object of charity, and other sources of information will uphold Mrs. Adams's statement.

In the light of this revelation, the story of Mrs. Blennerhassett's ambition to shine at the Court of St. James, and in other ways which would have brought her into the limelight, falls of its own weight. There is nothing to sustain the oft-repeated statement that she urged her husband on, other than the loyal devotion, so characteristic of her, to always unite her effort with his in whatever he undertook, though she was regarded as his superior in every way. With her heavy heart, her haunting fear, her crushed mother-hopes, as she watched the development of her children what could Ambition promise?

Mrs. Adams says that the shadow ever followed her, but that the social standing of her sisters, who demanded recognition for her in the homeland, helped in some measure to relieve the situation during her later residence in England—in her widowhood, at least.

The want of judgment that characterized Harman Blennerhassett in this fatal step, seemed to govern every act of his entire life. At every turn of the road, he seemed to take his destiny into his own hands and run away with it. There is no doubt that he had much book learning, but his stupidity was so marked, and his common sense so scarce that one almost stands amazed at his childlike acts. He seemed to be a man of good principles and of a high sense of honor, and he did not appear to have the least consciousness of wrong doing in the whole Burr affair—was open and frank in his entire proceedings.

History must agree with the verdict of the Wood County people. As stated by Woodbridge in the trial he is "considered a man of every other kind of sense but common sense," and thus the mantle of charity is thrown about Harman Blennerhassett. Small wonder that the gravestone inscription beseeches the "Stranger to pause and drop a tear."

Margaret Agnew, by this youthful misstep, evidently ruined an otherwise beautiful and useful life, for it cannot be denied that she was a superior woman; a woman of poise and character, and all the whispers of her disloyalty at the coming of Burr must fall for the want of the slightest proof to sustain them. Let us drop a flower of sympathy upon her vault and trust that the Island she loved may one day "blossom and bloom as the rose" under circumstances that may command the blessing of high Heaven in lasting beauty and glory.

16

Continuous Ownership of the Island
before and after
The Blennerhassetts

It has been said repeatedly that Colonel George Washington in his inspection tour down the Ohio, with his attendants in 1770, set this Island apart, by tomahawk title, as his own. But, if this be true, his journal overlooks it, and there seems to be no record proof to substantiate the claim. Other early stories cannot be verified in the light of the research of today. But the unexpected unearthing of the two deeds entitled, "Herron to Backus," and "Backus to Blennerhassett," in 1938, just about supplies the heretofore missing details of these transactions, and makes the matter clear.

According to these deeds, which are found in Deed Book 7, page 95, Wood County Records, there was a mercantile firm at Richmond, Virginia, known as the House of Nelson, Herron & Company, which was made up of the following personnel: John Wilcocks, of Philadelphia; Nicholas Law, of New York; Alexander Nelson, of Richmond; and James Herron, of Norfolk, Virginia, who on May 17, 1784, all came to an agreement that the power of handling the property of the company, should be vested in James Herron in absolute fee.

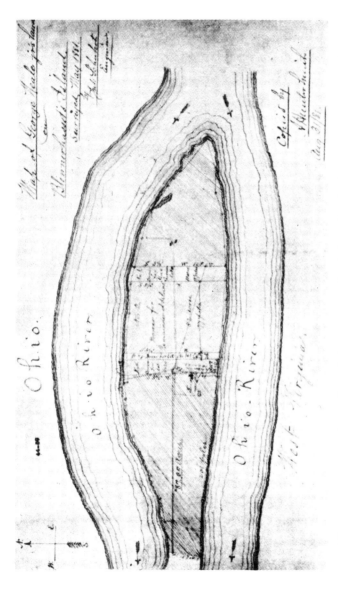

This map gives a clear idea of the upper end of the Island, the exact tract owned by Blennerhassett, which is now owned by Amos K. Gordon

Blockhouse and Log Cabins on Corn Island, 1778
First Settlement at Louisville, Kentucky

(From a ground plan by George R. Clark)

As this plan was so generally used in those early days, the one
on the Island is supposed to have been of this same pattern.

On May 15, 1786, Patrick Henry, the governor of the commonwealth of Virginia, granted the Island first below and next the mouth of the Little Kanawha River in the Ohio in Monongalia County—later Harrison, and next Wood—to Alexander Nelson in fee in trust for the Nelson, Herron & Company, and James Herron was authorized to sell and dispose of this real estate for the Company. On May 15, 1792, Herron sold it to Elijah Backus. It seems to have been distinctly two islands at that time. The first one is described as containing two hundred and ninety-seven acres; and the second one, two hundred and sixty-nine acres, and Backus paid two hundred and fifty pounds in Virginia currency. Henry Banks is given as assignee for Alexander Nelson, and John Harvie (?) and Samuel McDowell had been in turn assignees before.

In March, 1797, Elijah Backus and his wife, Hannah, sold the first Island below the mouth of the Little Kanawha, to Harman Blennerhassett and Joseph L. Lewis, of Philadelphia, merchant. This deed shows that this is the same tract that Patrick Henry granted to Alexander Nelson in trust for Nelson, Herron & Company—that it is the upper and eastern end of the Island. It also shows that the Island is to be for the sole use of Blennerhassett and his heirs, when he meets certain obligations to Joseph L. Lewis. So this may explain why Lewis became the owner of the Island after Blennerhassett, for we find evidence elsewhere that Lewis

demanded the sale of the Island to save his own interests. And in 1816 he became the sole owner.

It seems that Robert Miller, of Lexington, Kentucky,
who held the Island under writ of elegit from 1807 to
1816, must have been one of Blennerhassett's creditors;
for the Wood County records show that he secured judgment against Blennerhassett for the sum of $4,000 with
additional damages and interest in two cases, and
writs of elegit were afterwards issued by said court
and sheriff. David Putnam, of Marietta, Ohio, was
attorney for Miller, who later became a merchant at
Philadelphia. See Deed books 5, page 387; and 6, page
54, Wood County records.

Joseph L. Lewis, as early as 1820, turned the Island,
with all its claims, over to Thomas Morris and Samuel
Cauley for the purpose of disposing of it with all
speed, and at the best terms possible. Cauley died in
the meantime, and on December 31, 1827, we find
Thomas Morris transferring it by deed to George Neale,
junior, of Wood County for $2,500 in "lawful silver."
This deed is signed by Thomas Morris, Joseph L. Lewis
and his wife, Frances Lewis; and is found in Deed Book
7, page 125, Wood County. It is an unusually interesting document because of its informative nature, which
includes so much history of the former transactions and
ownership of the Island. It verifies again the title of
the Blennerhassetts and the indenture which records
their deed to Joseph L. Lewis; graphically describes the

Island, as "the first one in the Ohio below the mouth of the Little Kanawha, known as the name of Blennerhassett Island, and containing by estimate two hundred acres more or less," as shown in Deed Book 5, page 278, under date of April 11, 1817, Wood County records.

George Neale, who calls himself the elder in his will, was the tenant of the Island, 1811, when it was burned. His son, George Neale, junior, who was destined to become the future owner of the historic spot, then a child of nine, was in the house at the time and ever remembered the excitement of that hour, which was brought about by the upsetting of a candle midst the revelry of the slaves. George Neale, junior, was the builder of the old brick house of the Island of today, in 1833, which stands as a monument to his memory.

For further story of the ownership of the Island, we turn to Will Book 7, page 315, to the "Last Will and Testament" of George Neale, junior, under date of March 18, 1868, where he speaks of his "Island Farm"; and in Codicil second, May 16, 1870, where he stipulates, that after the death of his second wife, Agnes R. Neale, his Blennerhassett Island Farm be sold, and the proceeds invested in the interest of his daughter, Alice Neale, who is the wife of Amos W. Gordon, whom he names as his executor in his final codicil.

But Agnes R. Neale, his widow, was not willing to abide by his will, so we turn to a suit in chancery, following his death in 1880, Order Book 7, page 321, where she brings suit for partition of the estate, and asks that her dower be placed in the Island. And in the decision handed down in August, 1881, her request is granted, and her dower is vested in lots 1, 2, 3, and 4 in the Island. This suit discloses that George Neale, junior, had, in June, 1879, already deeded thirty-three acres of the Island Farm to his daughter, Alice—Mrs. Amos W. Gordon—and the mother would hold her dower rights in this, also. So the will was thus set aside, and Joseph P. Neal became the administrator of the estate. So for more than one hundred and ten years the Island has remained in the hands of George Neale, junior, and his direct descendants. The lower eighty-seven acres strayed from the family ownership for fifty-four years, but were bought back by Amos K. Gordon, in 1935; but the upper one hundred and forty acres, the entire historic portion, including mansion site, well, etc., to the extreme head of the island, has never been out of the family since 1827. This is the whole tract— now estimated at two hundred and twenty-seven acres —owned by Blennerhassett; and Amos K. Gordon, grandson of George Neale, junior, is the sole owner, and the restorer of the Island.

As we already know, Blennerhassett built the mansion in accord with the architectural plans of Colonel Joseph Barker, of Marietta, ancestor of Doctor Oliver D. Barker, of Parkersburg, and the Marietta Barkers, and his portrait hangs upon the museum walls at

Marietta, in confirmation of this distinction. The will of George Neale, "the elder of Washington Bottom," as found in Will Book 4, page 361, January 15, 1851, is an important contribution to Wood County history. It discloses, among other things, that William H. Safford, the author of the "Life of Harman Blenner-hassett," published in 1850, and later editor of the "Blennerhassett Papers," was the son-in-law of George Neale, the elder, as he married Ann Pocahontas Neale, and both are named as beneficiaries of the will. He also includes his granddaughter, Sarah E. Creel, wife of William L. Jackson, who was the daughter of Henry Clay and Lucy Neale Creel. Sarah Neale, wife of the testator, is also mentioned in the will, which was recorded in 1854; as is George Neale, junior, the later owner of the Island.

The Museum at Marietta has some beautiful pieces of furniture from the Blennerhassett Mansion—among them being a desk of mahogany and walnut; and a cherry-wood chair. Then there are wax candles, and the old keys found in the debris in the wine cellar. On the wall hangs the portrait of General Edward Tupper, who inscribed his name in the tragedy of the mansion.

Blennerhassett was qualified as justice of the peace for Wood County in 1799, the records show; and he took the oath of Allegiance and became a naturalized citizen of the United States in 1803.

17

Elijah Backus

Elijah Backus was an individual of some importance, aside from his ownership of the Island. His forebears came from Norwich, England, as early as 1637 and settled in Connecticut. He was the son of Elijah Backus I and Lucy Griswold Backus, who had a number of other children. James Backus, born 1764, brother of Elijah Backus, junior, was appointed as one of the early surveyors of the Northwest Territory, and arrived at the mouth of the Muskingum in June, 1788. His house was one of the first temporary ones to be erected in this Northwest Territory, one hundred and fifty years ago. Lucy Backus, sister of Elijah, junior, and James Backus, married Dudley Woodbridge I, and was the mother of Dudley Woodbridge II, the business partner of Blennerhassett. The Woodbridges joined the little colony at the mouth of the Muskingum in 1789. Elijah Backus, junior, came in 1790.

Elijah Backus, junior, born May 2, 1759, was graduated from Yale in 1777 and entered the profession of law. He was the editor of the "Ohio Gazette and the Territorial and Virginia Herald," the first newspaper published in Washington County, Ohio, in December, 1801, and two years later he became the owner of the paper. He later sold it to Samuel Fairlamb.

He was a candidate for the Ohio State Senate in 1803. But we find him as a citizen of Kaskaskia, Indiana Territory in 1806 and the Ohio Gazette of October 28, 1811, notices his death, while he was acting as receiver of Public Monies in the Land Office at Kaskaskia. He was married in 1784 to Miss Lucretia Hubbard, who died on February 17, 1787, leaving two children, Thomas Backus, and Lucretia, who later became the wife of Judge Nathaniel Pope, of Kaskaskia Both have descendants scattered through Ohio and the West to-day.

Backus Lived on the Island

The romantic story of the first part of the Island— now known as the upper end, has so completely overshadowed the lower end that few have ever known that Backus settled on that part of the Island, where he must have been living when he sold the "first Island" to Blennerhassett. The second Island or lower end contained two hundred and sixty-nine acres, as shown by the deeds; and Backus bought it, along with the upper end in 1792. Old family letters tell us that Elijah Backus was "captivated by the Island." It is referred to in these letters as "Elijah's Island—a delightful bit of verdure set in the Ohio River, about twelve miles west of Marietta." And it is these letters that tell us that he built upon the Island and removed to it. His sister,

Mrs. Lucy Woodbridge, writes to home folks in Connecticut, May, 1793, thus:

"Brother Elijah's situation has become quite Elijahable—he is now building upon the Island." In 1797, "Elijah has removed to his Island and lives as independently as a Prince." One of these letters in describing the Island, says,

"It is a situation that affords every amusement that a spot of ground can do without society. At one end of the island is a thick wood of about fifty acres, excellent hunting ground, which is cut off in winter by the water from the river, which forms smooth ice for skating; at the other extreme is a cove that at all seasons produces fish in great abundance of every kind. He has a beach in summer, which affords an excellent road for a carriage and horses, and which extends the length of the island— the whole of which is beautifully situated in the river, and affords many elegant building spots. He has likewise a sugar orchard . . ." This was the same year that Backus sold the upper end of the Island to Blennerhassett. So we glimpse Backus' love for the Island. But on April 24, 1807, after he had removed to Kaskaskia, in Indiana Territory, he sold this lower Island to Aaron Waldo Putnam, of Belpre, Ohio.*

This end of the Island, too, has had its changes and vicissitudes through the years. Rathvon Van Winkle bought a portion of it at a forced sale in 1859, and he

*See Deed Book 4, page 3, Wood County Records.

sold to Albert Logan* in 1864, and Howe and Hutchinson, the Logan heirs, still own this one hundred twenty-one acres, which joins Amos K. Gordon at the second Woods. The lower portion of one hundred forty-one acres is owned by Dr. Horace D. Price and the Dudley heirs.

*See Deed Book 22, page 267, Wood County Records.

Note—For Backus Story, as above, see Woodbridge-Gallaher Collection, Library of the Ohio State Archaeological and Historical Society. Also the Ohio State Archaeological and Historical Quarterly, Volume 44, Number 4, 1935.

Note—This research has involved much time and care, and we are confident that it is as nearly correct as is possible to give it. It will be noted that the Herron and Blennerhassett deeds, which appear in Deed Book 7, page 95, Wood County records, have some errors by the copyist; for it was not Wood County then; and Blennerhassett bought the island in 1797—not 1799.

"The Deserted Isle"

By Margaret Agnew Blennerhassett

"Like mournful echo from the silent tomb,
That pines away upon the midnight air,
While the pale moon breaks out with fitful gloom
Fond memory turns with sad, but welcome care,
To scenes of desolation and despair;
Once bright with all that beauty could bestow,
That peace could shed or youthful fancy know.

"To the fair Isle, reverts the pleasing dream,
Again thou risest in thy green attire,
Fresh, as at first, thy blooming graces seem;
Thy groves, thy fields, their wonted sweets respire;
Again thou'rt all my heart could e'er desire.
O! why, dear Isle, art thou not still my own?
Thy charms could then for all my griefs atone.

"The stranger that descends Ohio's stream,
Charm'd with the beauteous prospects that arise,
Marks the soft isles that, 'neath the glittering beam,
Dance with the wave and mingle with the skies,
Sees, also, one that now in ruin lies,
Which erst, like fairy queen, towered o'er the rest,
In every native charm, by culture, dress'd.

"There rose the seat, where once, in pride of life,
My eye could mark the queenly river's flow,
In summer's calmness or in winter's strife,
Swollen with rains or battling with the snow.
Never, again, my heart such joy shall know.
Havoc, and ruin, rampant war, have pass'd
Over that isle with their destroying blast.

"The black'ning fire has swept throughout her halls
The winds fly whistling o'er them and the wave
No more in spring-floods, o'er the sand-beach crawls,
But furious drowns in one o'erwhelming grave,
Thy hallowed haunts it watered as a slave.
Drive on, destructive flood! and ne'er again
On that devoted isle let man remain.

"Too many blissful moments there I've known,
Too many hopes have there met their decay;
Too many feelings now forever gone,
To wish that thou couldst ere again display
The joyful coloring of thy prime array;
Buried with thee, let them remain a blot,
With thee, their sweets, their bitterness forgot.

"And oh! that I could wholly wipe away
The memory of the ills that worked thy fall;
The memory of that all-eventful day,
When I return'd and found my own fair hall
Held by the infuriate populace in thrall,
My own fireside blockaded by a band
That once found food and shelter of my hand.

"My children, oh! a mother's pangs forbear,
Nor strike again that arrow to my soul;
Clasping the ruffians in suppliant prayer,
To free their mother from unjust control,
While with false crimes and imprecations foul,
The wretched, vilest refuse of the earth,
Mock jurisdiction held around my hearth.

"Sweet isle! methinks I see thy bosom torn;
Again behold the ruthless rabble throng
That wrought destruction taste must ever mourn.
Alas! I see thee now, shall see thee long;
But ne'er shall bitter feelings urge the wrong,
That, to a mob, would give the censure due
To those that arm'd the plunder-greedy crew."

*   *   *   *   *

Old Neale Brick House, taken 1921 by Author

PART II

Burr Under Footlights and Shadows
Tragedy of the Beautiful Theodosia

To Theodosia Burr
whose life of intermingled
joy and sorrow has touched
the heart of a world.

I dream'd I lay where flowers were springing
Gayly in the sunny beam;
Listening to the wild birds singing,
By a fallen crystal stream.
Straight the sky grew black and daring,
Thro the woods the whirlwinds rave,
Trees with aged arms were warring,
O'er the swelling drumlie wave,
Such was Life's deceitful morning.

—Robert Burns

From Stuart Portrait *Original owned by Annie Burr Jennings*

Theodosia Burr as a Child

Summer home of Alstons in South Carolina
where "little Gamp" died

Copy of shell painting owned by Mrs. F. W. Ford,
Georgetown, South Carolina, great-grand niece
of Joseph Alston

1

Burr—from Cradle to Manhood

We have followed the Blennerhassetts to the end of the trail. Now let us turn to Burr with soft pedals on our prejudices, and briefly review his career before and after misfortune turned his glory into lengthening shadows.

Aaron Burr came of distinguished ancestry. His forbears on both sides had stamped the impress of sturdy characters and religious fervor in Colonial history and had set a high standard for their descendants to follow long before his time. His maternal grandsire, the Reverend Jonathan Edwards, who traced back through the Tuthills in direct line to Alfred the Great, was one of the most illustrious divines that America has produced. His father, the Reverend Aaron Burr, D.D., lives in history as one of the founders of Princeton University, as well as an eminent divine. He had been pastor of the First Presbyterian Church at Newark, New Jersey, for fifteen years when he summoned the beautiful Esther Edwards, then eighteen, to the manse for the nuptials. Of this novel affair, she writes thus in her journal:

"The good man that has chosen me for his bride has sent a young messenger from Newark, with two horses, to conduct my honored mother and myself to New

Jersey. He says 'there is plenty of Scripture for it. Did
not Isaac thus send for Rebecca'? I am to ride Nimrod,
Mr. Burr's great admiration and pride. I am so glad
to go. I suppose I feel some as Christiana in 'Pilgrim's
Progress' when she had to follow her husband. . . . I
had to kiss the bark of the elm tree that stands in front
of my window, and where I have so often watched the
returning robins, as they built their nests and reared
their young, and taught them to fly away; and now, I
am to stretch my wings and go after their example. But
mine are the wings of the dove." As she mounts the
hill on Nimrod and casts lingering glances at the loveliness of the village below where she has spent so many
happy hours, she closes her eyes that she may ever retain
this picture. But Nimrod, in his eagerness to bear her to
his Master, then gives her plenty to do without more
dreaming.

The Reverend Aaron Burr and Esther Edwards were
married on June 9, 1752, and while their nuptial years
were to be few, they were very happy ones. Mr. Burr
was a number of years older, but she evidently adored
him. Once in writing a friend after three years of wedded
life, she said, "Do you think I would change my good
Mr. Burr for any person, or thing, or all things on the
earth? No sure! not for a million such worlds as this,
yt had no Mr. B——r in it." In making comparison
between her distinguished father and her husband, she
said, "I think my father more impressive and solemn;

but Mr. Burr is more ingratiating and captivating; has more of what people call eloquence."

But it was the small bundle of masculinity that was laid in the cradle at the manse at Newark on February 6, 1756 that is of more moment to us, though these parents are most interesting. The first glimpse that we have of this youngster, who was named for his father, is through the eyes of his mother, who has left this notation in her journal:

"Aaron is a little, dirty, noisy boy, very different from Sally, almost in everything. He begins to talk a little, is very sly, mischievous, and has more sprightliness than Sally. I must say that he is handsomer, but not so good-tempered. He is very resolute and requires a good governor to bring him to terms." The father entertained the idea that four-year-old Sally Burr might be styled a "numb-head" when she started to school, but the mother's journal estimate of little Sally is, "just about middling in all accounts."

Burr's father became the president of Princeton University shortly after his birth, and the family removed from Newark to Princeton, where the father was soon laid away in the cemetery. The Reverend Aaron Burr died on September 24, 1757 in his forty-second year. His father-in-law, the Reverend Jonathan Edwards, succeeded him as head of Princeton, but he followed Mr. Burr across the sundown slope within a few months, from fever due to inoculation from smallpox, and

Death did not stop here. Sixteen days later, on April 7, 1758, Mrs. Burr was laid in her casket from the same malady, and the two children, so sadly bereaved, were taken to relatives in Philadelphia.

By and by the grandmother, Mrs. Sarah Edwards, went to bring them home to live with her, but Death suddenly overtook her. Thus within the brief period of thirteen months these little ones had been deprived of both parents and grandparents; and four-year old Sarah Burr, and her little two-year-old brother, Aaron, were left to the care of their uncle, Timothy Edwards, whose home was at Elizabethtown, New Jersey.

Timothy Edwards is described as a cold, Puritanical, severe man, who did not believe in "sparing the rod and spoiling the child," and little Aaron was unhappy with him, and repeatedly ran away. It is told that the child took offense at his tutor when he was but four years old, and hid himself away so as to elude search for several days. At eight, we find him concealed in a cherry tree in his uncle's garden, showering the ripe fruit down upon the rare frock of an elderly lady, whose straight-laced ideas had won his displeasure on former visits to the Edwards home, and who now promptly reported the vandal act to that stern uncle, who summoned the lad to his study where the staid, Puritan discipline was applied. First, a lecture on the enormity of the offense; then a long petition on bended knees for the reformation of the offender; then the rod. "He licked me like a sack," was Burr's version of the interview in after years.

At the age of ten, the lad ran away a second time; going to New York where he enlisted as cabin boy on board a ship which was preparing for sea. One day he spied his uncle coming on board, and hastily scaled the heights to the mast head out of reach. When the austere man in clerical robe ordered him to come down, he refused to obey; the command softened into entreaty, and finally into negotiation, with the promise that if he would come down and return to his studies that there would be no disagreeable sequel. Upon these terms the little rebel went home with his pious uncle.

But there was some sunshine in the life of the little orphan, despite the severity of the rod. For the boy loved the great outdoors. Fishing, rowing, hunting, horseback riding, and his books. At the age of eleven he was ready for college, but when he knocked at Princeton for admission, it was denied him "owing to his age and inches"; for he was almost diminutive in size. He was admitted to the sophomore class, two years later, however, and came out with honors. Despite his frolicsome nature, he learned with a rapidity that has seldom been surpassed.

Heredity had naturally mapped out a theological course for him, and after Princeton, came a tryout at the study of theology, but he could not accept a doctrine that did not leave the way open to Heaven for all alike;

so he laid down his theology, suspended judgment on religion, and turned his attention to the study of law. In the meantime, his sister, Sally Burr, had been married to Tappan Reeve, her tutor, and he went into his brother-in-law's office at Litchfield, Connecticut. He had already begun his youthful flirtations at Princeton, and there were just as pretty girls in Connecticut. One of these was Dorothy Quincy, of Boston, whom he had met at Fairfield in the summer, and who, Tradition hints, might have preferred the debonair young lawyer to John Hancock had she been permitted to enjoy his society without the guardianship of a chaperon.

However, in July, 1775, the "guns of Lexington" called Young Burr with thousands of others into the Continental Army. He was one of Arnold's brave six hundred on the expedition to Canada that same year. His courage and determination on this fatiguing march so won the admiration of Arnold that he gave him a letter of introduction and commendation to General Montgomery. Burr, now but nineteen, found himself on Montgomery's staff on November 20, 1775, and on the day of the fateful battle, Captain Burr with the first division marched at his General's side. "We shall be in the fort within two minutes"! Montgomery exclaimed to Burr. But a deafening roar of artillery came just then, and Montgomery was dying in a staff officer's arms. Burr and a French guide alone of the men at the head of the column remained alive. Arnold was wounded, and his second in command, captured.

Montgomery lay dead in the snow, and Burr returned to the spot through grave dangers determined to rescue the body, but it was too heavy for so slight a youth. The fame of Burr's gallantry in this expedition went before him to New York, and upon his return there was a place awaiting him on the staff of General Washington, who was encamped in the very old mansion at Richmond Hill that Burr was to make famous years afterwards. Captain Burr worked on the orderly books of the Commander-in-Chief, but their natures jarred, and within a short time, the youthful Hero went over to the staff of General Putnam where he was happier, despite the tempestuous nature of this old Warrior. It was Major Burr who was sent to Long Island in August, 1776, to do duty under General McDougal, and who rescued the brigade of General Knox after the disaster at Long Island. His entire military record was gallant, patriotic, and praiseworthy. But owing to failing health, he was compelled to resign, 1779, and he returned to the study of law, the following year, and was admitted to the bar at Albany two years later.

2

Burr in Romance and Homelife

Romance and the well-written billet-doux had a peculiar charm for Aaron Burr, and his power to sway hearts is one of the fixed and indisputable features of his many biographies with their varied interpretations. Frivolity did not appeal to him. He admired the interesting woman whether she belonged in palace or cottage, and the announcement of his marriage to a woman, at least ten years older than himself, without wealth or beauty, and with a slight facial disfigurement from a burn, and partially an invalid, created no small stir in social circles where he had been courted and flattered by the mothers of some of the fairest belles of the land.

During his service in the American Revolution, Burr had met Mrs. Theodosia Bartow Prevost, at Paramus, New Jersey, the widow of Mark Prevost, a native of Switzerland, who lost his life as an officer in the British Army on the Island of Jamaica, 1779. She was the daughter and only child of Attorney Theodosius Bartow, and Anne Stillwell Bartow, who later became Mrs. De Visne, and she had two sons, Frederick A. J. and John Bartow Prevost. Their courtship as disclosed in their letters was an unusual one. He "loved her because she had the truest heart, the ripest intellect, and the most winning and graceful manners of any woman that he had ever met." They were married on July 6, 1782, and their romance did not end with their honeymoon, but it was one of those rare companionships of mind and heart that will not brook separation. A feeling of sadness steals over us as we think of the pain occasioned by these enforced separations, but history would have lost one of its most delightful glimpses into the home-life of married lovers, had it not been for the letters, which bridged the chasm of these separations. Here are a few extracts from that adoring wife:

"My Aaron had scarce quitted the door when I regretted my passiveness. Why did I consent to his departure? . . . my Aaron, dark is the hour that separates my soul from itself . . . Heaven protect my Aaron; preserve him, restore him to his adoring mistress . . . Love in all its delirium hovers about me; like opium, it lulls me to soft repose! Sweet serenity speaks, 'tis my Aaron's spirit presides. Surrounding objects check my visionary charm. I fly to my room and give the day to thee." Then again, we read:

"I pursued thee yesterday through wind and rain till eve when fatigued, exhausted, shivering, thou didst reach thy haven, surrounded by inattention, thy Theo far from thee . . . I beheld my much loved Aaron, his tender eyes fixed on me . . . This soothed my troubled spirit; I slept tolerably, but dare not trust too confidently . . . naught but thy voice can tran- quilize my mind. Thou art the constant subject of love,

hope, fear." Burr's letters to her during his enforced
absences from home were masterpieces in their combined
affection, wit, and helpful intelligence. There are few,
if any, on record that can compare with them. Ten
years after they had plighted their troth, we hear him
saying, "It was knowledge of your mind, which
first inspired me with respect for that (mind) of your
sex."

On July 23, 1783, a beautiful little daughter came
to crown their homelife with a fuller measure of com-
pleteness. No father ever trained a daughter with more
care, and no daughter ever gave to a father more tender
devotion. His admiration for the adornment of mind
in woman seemed to tower over all else, and he omitted
nothing in her education and training that was calculated to bring out his highest ideal of womanhood.
He was not in sympathy with the idea of woman being
woman just because she was thus born. He believed that
education and culture should be a part of her development. He seemed to glimpse in the distance the first
rays of the dawn of the new sunrise for woman, and
unwittingly made his own loved daughter an exponent
of it. His part as a father seemed to transcend every
other quality that he possessed, and if he wished Theodosia to be the equal of man intellectually, his superior
morally, pure, proud, courageous, self-poised, beautiful,
gentle, and gracious, he surely felt no disappointment in
the outcome. For she was without doubt one of the

best educated women of her time. Once during a pro-longed absence from home, he wrote to his wife, "Cursed effects of fashionable education of which both sexes are the advocates and yours, the victims. If I could foresee that Theo would become a mere fashionable woman, with whatever grace or allurement, I would earnestly pray God to take her forthwith hence." Sally, another little daughter, like a frail flower, brightened their home for a brief time, then faded and died. His step-sons were members of the household, and students in his office, and in him they found an interested father.

During the autumn of 1783, Burr transferred his home and law practice from Albany to New York City, and finally came into possession of historic old Richmond Hill, which was often thronged with the elite of the day, for he was now in the United States Senate, and his brilliancy was winning for him a name. But in the midst of his triumphs, a great shadow fell across the threshold of Richmond Hill when the wife, who had inspired his deepest devotion, slipped away on May 18, 1794, after a long invalidism, during his absence. Aaron Burr turned from her grave another man. Up to this time, his entire life had been wholesome and admirable, aside from his youthful escapades under stern dictator-ship. His homelife had been ideal, but all was to be changed now—that gentle influence of which he loved to speak in after years had been removed, and Aaron Burr was like some rudderless vessel.

Theodosia was now but eleven years of age, but her training and education had fitted her for usefulness and helpfulness even at this tender age. She could entertain her father's guests, and often translated his documents into French. But when she was a little older, he admitted to his home Natalie de L'age, a French girl, who is styled as his adopted daughter by some historians, that Theodosia might have the advantage of conversing in French, and the helpfulness of the companionship. They together played the hostess for Richmond Hill, and added new romances to its interesting history.

When Robert Livingston went as minister to France, Natalie de L'age accompanied the party, as did Thomas Sumpter, son of General Sumpter, of South Carolina, who had been appointed as secretary of the legation. When the vessel arrived over rough seas in Paris, she became the bride of Thomas Sumpter, who was later made minister plenipotentiary to Brazil, where he served for ten years.

Theodosia Burr has now reached the age when she is surrounded by many admirers. In writing her father on one occasion she says:

"I might have had a little court of gentlemen, but this sort of admiration, which is excited by trifles, is not worth the price that must be paid for it. The good-will of my own sex is preferable, and a certain reserve, respectable. I therefore received few male visitors, and did not encourage them to return often." But Theodosia had one lover, who held her fast.

Aaron Burr and Richmond Hill

Theodosia and Natalie
at Richmond Hill

3

Theodosia's Romance and Marriage

Joseph Alston, a young lawyer of South Carolina, is the favored suitor for her hand, but when he asks her to name the day, she suggests indefinite postponement, which calls forth a most eloquent appeal in his own behalf under date of December 28, 1800, which begins:

"Hear me, Miss Burr" and extends into a veritable document, which discloses that he is now a young man of twenty-two with ample fortune; that he is passionately in love with a young lady almost eighteen, who has admitted a sincere friendship for him, and he can't accept the necessity of waiting, when the families on both sides are pleased with the attachment. He says, "From my father's plan of education for me, I may be properly called a hot-bed plant. Introduced from my infancy into the society of men, while yet a boy, I was accustomed to think and act like a man. On every occasion, however important, I was left to decide for myself. I do not recall a single instance when I was controlled by even advice; for it was my father's inviolable maxim that the best way of strengthening the judgment was to suffer it to be constantly exercised. Before seventeen, I finished my college education; before twenty, was admitted to the bar. Since that time I have been continually traveling through different

parts of the United States—to what purpose I leave
you to determine." He leaves her now to judge for
herself whether his sentiments and manners are not
in some degree formed. But letters traveled very slowly
in those days, and before this one had time to reach its
destination, the young lady, under date of January 13,
1801 pens him that she yields her judgment to his
solicitations, and the happy lover starts northward.

Aaron Burr is now a member of the New York
legislature, and Theodosia is at Albany with him. On
February 7, 1801, the New York Commercial Adver-
tiser carries the announcement of the wedding thus:

"Married—At Albany on 2d instant, by the Reverend Mr. Johnson, Joseph Alston, of South Carolina
to Theodosia Burr, only child of Aaron Burr, Esq."

The honeymoon was spent at Albany and Richmond
Hill, and on February 28, they joined Colonel Burr at
Baltimore and went on to Washington where they
attended the inaugural ceremonies on March 4, which
made Colonel Burr the vice president of the United
States. And then continued on to South Carolina where
they founded their home at The Oaks, a delightful old
plantation, which had been an ancestral inheritance of
Mr. Alston. Thus this queenly northern flower was
transplanted to the sodden fields of a southern plantation, where the atmosphere was not conducive to
health. And Richmond Hill and the heart of the fond
Father were empty. He tells her in an early letter, "I

approached my home as I would approach the sepulchre of all my friends. Dreary, solitary, comfortless. It was no longer home." Life was now an empty void, save for the comfort of the letters, and the hope of meeting that spanned the distance.

Let us go with Theodosia to her new home and learn something of her surroundings and the family in the background.

The Alstons were among the first settlers in Georgetown County, South Carolina. William Alston died in 1743, leaving a large family of children; and it was his son, Joseph Alston, who founded The Oaks. And at his death, he willed it to his grandson and namesake, who was then but a small lad, with the injunction that this grandson must have a liberal education. William Alston and his wife, Mary Ashe, who was the daughter of General Ashe, after whom Asheville, North Carolina took its name, were the parents of Joseph Alston, the husband of Theodosia Burr.

The injunction of his grandfather's will was carried out, and Joseph Alston, the younger, was well educated; and studied law in the office of Edward Rutledge, one of the signers of the Declaration of Independence. He began the practice of law, but having a large fortune, turned his attention to politics instead, and was elected to the legislature of South Carolina at a youthful age, became speaker of the house, and governor of the state, in 1812. Colonel Burr is said to have influenced him to turn his career into the political; for he was brilliant, amiable in manner, fluent in debate, and wielded his pen with as much ease in poetry as in prose.

Theodosia was very happy in her new surroundings, and to add to her joys, a wonderful son was born the first year of her wedded life. Her cup of happiness was now full. As soon as she was able to travel, she took the child and went to visit her father in New York, but the separation from her husband was most painful. In one of her letters she assures him "where you are, there is my country, and in you are centered all of my wishes." Then again, "You do not know how constantly my whole mind is employed in thinking of you. Do you, my husband, think as frequently of your Theo, and wish for her? Do you really feel a vacuum in your pleasures? As for your wife, she has bid adieu to pleasure till next October. When will that month come? it appears to me a century off. God knows how delighted I shall be when once again in your arms. When we meet, let there be nothing to alloy a happiness so pure, so unbounded. Our little boy grows charmingly. He is much admired here. The color of his eyes is not yet determined. You shall know when it is."

Another time, "Ah, my husband, what can be pleasure to your Theo, unassisted by the charm of your presence and participation? Nothing! It is an idea which has no place in my mind unconnected with you."

It has been said that she loved Washington Irving, and that her father brought about her union with Mr. Alston for political and financial reasons, but in the face of these letters and other proof of her unbounded devotion for her husband, and with the pathetic story of Irving's undying affection for the beautiful Matilda Hoffman whom he loved and lost in her youth, we may as well set aside this gossip for all time; for this was beyond all doubt a true love affair between Theodosia Burr and Joseph Alston, as much proof is still to come. In her earlier married life there seemed but little left to wish for. She was a most beloved wife; a proud mother, the adored daughter of a Vice President; a leader in the social world, beautiful, talented, wealthy, admired and petted as few women have ever been, and she seemed to realize how wonderfully she had been favored. But sad reverses awaited her, and we turn to the next chapter wishing that she might have been spared such crushing blows.

4

Against the Tide

As one quietly reviews the events of Burr's life in the light of to-day, there seems to be just one pivot upon which his entire destiny was hinged, and that was his rivalry with Alexander Hamilton.* They were both brilliant with kindred tastes and ambitions, but Burr's family background, and his early training naturally gave him the ascendancy over Hamilton, and he did not seem to find Hamilton in his way. However, this rivalry began back in Revolutionary days when they were young officers in the Continental Army, and it extended to almost every phase of their lives—even to the ball room, where Burr seemed to prevail with the fair one in question.

Unfortunately for both they shared the most important law practice in New York, and Hamilton was interested in Burr's defeat for governor of New York in 1792; then again, his influence played its part in President Washington's refusal to sanction Burr's appointment as minister to France when he had been the unanimous choice of his associates in Congress for that position. When Burr and Jefferson had tied in their vote for President of the United States, Hamilton again played well his part for Burr's defeat.

*See Beveridge's Version of Hamilton affair, "Life of John Marshall," Volume 3, footnote, pages 277-78.

Burr has sometimes been charged with discreditable methods in politics, but when the highest honor within the gift of his country was at stake, he surely belied such a charge; for "he would promise no patronage, pledge himself to no policy; was deaf to the impassioned importunities of his friends; and refused absolutely to influence one vote in his own behalf." And yet with such evidence in his favor, he has been branded as a traitor to his country for a century and a quarter.

But this election and its attendant circumstances revealed his popularity. Little Burr was seen to be a dangerous rival, not only by Hamilton, but the jealousy of other leaders had been aroused. In accord with his usual custom, Burr made no explanation of his course of procedure, offered no excuses, but from that moment he was doomed for overthrow. It mattered little how it was to be brought about, but such a dangerous rival must be removed. He now took his seat as Vice President of the United States, and added to his laurels by the grace and dignity with which he presided over the United States Senate—no vice president in history is classed above him. And it is recorded that he presided over the trial of Judge Chase in the Senate "with the dignity and impartiality of an angel and the rigor of a devil."

Burr had defeated Philip Schuyler, Hamilton's father-in-law, for the United States Senate, and Hamilton's hostility had burst out anew, before the Burr-Jefferson contest for President, and when Burr announced his candidacy for Governor of New York on the independent ticket, 1804, before the close of his tenure of office, as vice president, Hamilton sprang forth with more venom than ever. He seemed to call into play every underhand method for Burr's defeat; and it was for these underhand assaults during this heated campaign that Burr challenged him to duel. This "field of honor" which had the sanction of law, had been the common method of settling such matters; and more than one stalwart form had been laid low upon it. Jackson, Clay, Randolph, and Benton, had met their enemies within its arena, and why it should not have been as honorable for Burr, prejudice alone must answer.

But Hamilton seemed to be an idol with those high up in political circles, though history justifies the statement that he had some as grave faults as Burr, and the shot that ended his career on the field of Weehawken on July 11, 1804, was as truly fatal to Burr's. Just or unjust in this shot Burr sealed his future destiny. The enmity and jealousy that had already been gathering about him for the purpose of removing a brilliant and dangerous rival, now redoubled its effort. No praise was too great for the fallen; no denunciation, too severe for his destroyer.

A prejudiced indictment for murder drove him from New York, and his beloved Richmond Hill was sacrificed for debt. His thoughts on the eve of this duel naturally turned to the daughter he loved far more than all other earthly things, yet we see beneath it his thoughtful desire to protect her from pain. He virtually bids adieu to her and to earth, but outwardly all is calm, he does not tell her of the duel. But to her husband, he says:

"I have called out General Hamilton and we meet to-morrow. Van Ness will give you the particulars. The preceding has been written in contemplation of this event. If it shall be my lot to fall, yet, I shall live in you and your son. I commit to you all that is most dear to me—my reputation and my daughter. Your talents and your attachment will be the guardian of the one—your kindness and your generosity, of the other."

The duel took place. The next news that Theodosia received from her father, he was a fugitive from the abhorrence of his fellow citizens. An indictment for murder was hanging over him, his career was, perhaps, ended in New York. He was a wanderer upon the face of the earth. Ah! cruel message. Her happiness too was at an end. Her bright hopes had suddenly sunk into a night without even a star to relieve the density of its darkness. "She didn't censure; she didn't blame." She quietly accepted his version, and her confidence remained unshaken; her devotion, unfaltering. He had written her:

"Don't let me have the idea that you are dissatisfied with me at this moment. I can't just now endure it. At another time, you may play the Juno if you please."

"You will find the papers filled with all manner of nonsense and lies—accounts of attempts to assassinate me. These, I assure you, are mere fables. Those who wish me dead prefer to keep at a respectful distance." This was under date of August 3. Then on September 15, he writes her that he will be compelled to abandon the hope of seeing her until late in February, and continues:

"On this as on all other occasions, let me find that you exhibit the firmness, which I have been proud to ascribe to you."

It was at this time that he made his first brief tour of the South, and in October, 1804, contrary to his expectations, he met Theo and her husband, while on his way to Washington to preside over the United States Senate in December. He had now been indicted for murder in New Jersey, and while he treated the matter as a farce, it did not quiet her fears and forebodings, and her health suffered in consequence, despite his constant urging for her to be her self again, she fell into a decline.

But he completed his duties as vice president; and his farewell address to the Senate, so replete in pathos and eloquence, that it left that body in tears as the door closed behind him, still bears silent testimony to his surpassing ability and his dignity as a presiding official.

In his dilemma, he resolved to found a colony of his own, and purchased four hundred thousand acres on the banks of the Wabash, a tributary of the Red River, for this purpose, and again sailed down the Ohio with the dire results that we already know. Court and jury vindications, other want of testimony to convict played no part, his countrymen branded him as a traitor, and have held this verdict over him for a century and a quarter without one iota of fact to justify it.

It was while Theodosia was passing through this ordeal—torn between love and fear for her father, that she wrote the following letter to her husband, when she felt death near. It is dated August 5, 1805 and reads:

"To you, my beloved husband, I leave our child! the child of my bosom, who was once a part of myself, and from whom I shall shortly be separated by the cold grave. You love him now; henceforth love him for me also. And oh! my husband, attend to this last prayer of a doting mother. Never listen to what any other person tells you of him. Be yourself his judge on all occasions. He has faults, see them and correct them, yourself. Desist not an instant from your endeavors to secure his confidence. It is a work which requires as much unfaulty conduct as warmth of affection towards him. I know, my beloved, that you can perceive what is right on this subject as on every other. But recollect these are the last words I can ever utter. It will tranquilize my last moments to have disburdened myself of them. I fear you will scarcely be able to read this scrawl but I feel hurried and agitated.

"Death is not welcome. I confess it is ever dreaded. You have made me too fond of life. Adieu, then, thou kind, thou tender husband. Adieu! friend of my heart. May Heaven prosper you and may we meet hereafter. Adieu! perhaps we may never see each other again in this world. You are away. I wished to hold you fast, and prevent you from going this morning. But He who is wisdom, itself, ordains events! we must submit to them. Least of all should I murmur. I, on whom so many blessings have been showered; whose days have been numbered by bounties; who has such a husband; such a child; such a father. Oh! pardon me, my God, if I regret leaving these. I resign myself. Adieu! once more for the last time, my beloved. Speak of me often to our son. Let him love the memory of his mother, and let him know how he was loved by her.

"Your wife, your fond wife

Theo"

"P. S.—Let my father see my son sometimes. Do not be unkind towards him whom I have loved so much, I beseech you. Burn all my papers except my father's letters, which I beg you return to him. Adieu! my sweet boy, love your father; be grateful and affectionate to him while he lives; be the pride of his meridian; the support of his departing days. Be all that he wishes; for he made your mother happy. Oh! my heavenly Father, bless them both. If it is permitted, I will hover round you, and guard you, and intercede for you. I hope for happiness in the next world for I have not been bad in this."

But Theodosia did not die. She was spared for greater sorrows and trials; and this letter never reached her husband until she had gone from him into the mysteries of shadow.

The next awful message that reached her was that of the arrest of her father for treason against his country, and we have already followed her with her wonderful grace and fortitude through that fiery ordeal; for when he suffered, she suffered; when he triumphed, she triumphed, for her love and loyalty knew no caprice.

With the fear of the hangman and imprisonment now removed she returned to her home to face the social ostracism of her father, and to brave a new trial in his exile.

5

Burr's Exile and return to the Homeland

Burr found it necessary to remain incognito much of the time following the trial, and on June 7, 1808, he sailed for Europe under the name of Edwards. He found shelter in the meantime in the home of old friends in New York; and it was here, in the Pollock home, that he bade adieu to Theodosia, who came under the guise of his sister, Mary Ann Edwards, on the eve of his sailing. He carried with him the hope that his plan for the redemption of Mexico would yet meet with favor somewhere in Europe. But again disappointment awaited him, and suspicion followed in his footsteps. Distrust drove him from place to place and want often stared him in the face. He visited England, Scotland, Sweden, Holland, France, Germany, and back to England to sail for home, after four years of wandering. Despite the fact that American diplomats and others looked upon him with suspicion, he was oftentimes received into the best circles with cordiality.

But through all his reverses and wanderings, there was one heart that never failed him. His lovely daughter constantly wrote and cheered him, as he did her. The diary he kept, which has many stained and forbidden pages in it, gives one an insight into the inner chambers, when want and woe overwhelmed. With breaking heart,

Theodosia looked out from her varied places of retirement, eagerly watching—waiting for some sign of abatement in the feeling against her father. She realized that her social star had set; that few of her fair-weather friends remained; and in writing her father concerning this change, she said:

"The world begins to cool terribly around me. You would be surprised how many I supposed attached to me have abandoned the sorry, losing game of disinterested friendship."

But midst it all, her father was first. She urged his return, assuring him if he must suffer that she would suffer with him. She seemed just as willing to own him and to share his misfortune as she had been to share his honors. She repeatedly appealed to men high up in the councils of the nation, without the knowledge of her husband, in behalf of justice for her father. She could not comprehend why he should thus be persecuted and driven into exile, when his innocence had been established by law. He had introduced her to Mr. and Mrs. James Madison, and when Mr. Madison became President, she appealed to him, through the woman-heart of Dolly Madison, in order to determine whether prosecution further awaited his return; and her appeal to Albert Gallatin is a feminine masterpiece.

But when she finally did persuade her father to brook all danger and return to the homeland, almost insurmountable difficulties deferred his plans from time to time. Debts had to be paid; passports were delayed; penury was often his portion; enemies were combined, until conditions were sometimes desperate. Starvation threatened him at one time right in the great city of Paris. But whenever he had an extra shilling, he was collecting gifts for Theodosia or little Gamp, then again Adversity would see him pawn them. He began asking for passports, 1810, but it was not until March 26, 1812 that he actually sailed on the Aurora, which was to land him in Boston on the following May 4. While he was waiting for the unraveling of the governmental tape, he went to Holland, and in this hour of need he was compelled to part with the small watch that he had bought for little Gamp. How the tenderness of his inner nature is disclosed in the Journal confidence that parts him from this treasure:

"Putting it to my ear and kissing it and begging you a thousand pardons, you dear, little, beautiful watch was —was sold. I do assure you—but you know how sorry I was— . . . But heigho! when I get rich I will buy you a prettier one." (How fortunate that he did not know that little Gamp was never to need the watch!)

Having automatically changed from prince to pauper, as the circumstances demanded, while abroad, Burr was still equal to the occasion when the Aurora landed at Boston. He had gone away under the name of Edwards; he was returning as Mr. Arnot. As the vessel neared the landing, he wrote in his journal, "All is bustle and joy except Gamp. Why should he rejoice?" He remained in Boston under guise until May 30, and had to part with some books in order to secure passage to New York. He took the Rose sloop, little "teenty thing of forty tons" for New York, and on June 4, it was off the Mill River at Fairfield, Connecticut, where he had met Dorothy Quincy, later Mrs. John Hancock, and where every object was so familiar that he feared to stir lest he be recognized. For this reason, he declined the invitation of his cousin, Thaddeus Burr, to go fishing and shooting, but did venture for a stroll on shore that he might renew his acquaintance "with inanimate objects." Everything was as familiar to him as his own Richmond Hill, and he tells his journal,

"At several doors I saw the very lips I had kissed, the very eyes that had ogled me in the persons of their grandmothers, six and thirty years ago. I did not venture into any of their houses, lest some of the grandmothers might recollect me." He was obliged to continue his journey to New York in another vessel on June 8, 1812.

Burr always had friends—someone who believed in him, and he found them in New York upon his return. He possessed ten dollars in cash, and soon a little tin sign appeared at Number nine, Nassau Street, announcing that he would here resume the practice of law. He had hoped that this would bring returns enough for his daily needs, but clients flocked to his door and it took several clerks to meet the situation. It is said that

he made two thousand dollars within the first twelve
days. But scarcely had he begun to realize the turn of
fortune when two letters reached him from the South-
land, and the darkness of night was upon him again.

We read, "Little Gamp is dead!" The child about
whom so many fond hopes were entwined has been
laid beneath the summer flowers. The broken-hearted
father breathes forth his agony thus:

"One dreadful blow has destroyed us! That boy on
whom all rested . . . he who was to have redeemed
all your glory and shed new luster upon our families—
that at once our happiness and pride—is dead. We saw
him dead—yet we are alive . . . Theodosia has
endured all that a human could endure, but her admirable mind will triumph. She supported herself in a
manner worthy of your daughter."

Then we turn to the almost broken sentences of the
distracted mother:

"There is no more joy for me! the world is blank. I
have lost my boy! My child is gone forever. He expired
on June 30. Then again a month later:

"Alas! my father, I do live, but how, but how does
it happen? . . . Whichever way I turn, the same anguish assails me. You talk of consolation. Oh! you
know not what you have lost! I think Omnipotence
could give no equivalent for my boy! no! none—none!"

Again we read from the depth of the father's anguish:

"A few miserable weeks since, my dear sir, and in spite of all the embarrassment, the troubles and disappointments which have fallen to our lot, since we parted, I would have congratulated you upon your return in language of happiness. With my wife on one side and my boy on the other, I felt myself superior to depression. The present was enjoyed, the future was anticipated with enthusiasm. One dreadful blow has destroyed us; reduced us to the veriest, the most sublimated wretchedness. That boy on whom all rested; our companion, our friend; he who was to have transmitted down the mingled blood of Theo and myself— My own hand surrendered him to the grave. I will not conceal from you that life is a burden, which heavy as it is, we shall both support, if not with dignity, at least with decency and firmness."

6

Theodosia Lost at Sea

Theodosia had borne too much. She was now very ill, and her father insisted that she come to him. Just at this time our country was involved in its second war with Great Britain, and her husband, who was governor of the state, wrote Colonel Burr, that he was now in command as brigadier-general and awaiting employment against Quebec, should an army be sent there; that he had asked a brigade of the president, and that this held him fast—that he could not leave. Colonel Burr then sent his old friend, Timothy Greene from New York, to accompany her there, but he found her too ill for such a trip over land; and passage was secured for her and her maid and Mr. Greene on board the Patriot, a schooner-built pilot boat, which was in refitting at Georgetown, South Carolina. This vessel had discharged her privateer crew, hidden her armament beneath deck, and was preparing for a dash to New York with the fruitage of her raids under the ostensible covering of a cargo of rice. The time of her departure was known, and the danger was not concealed; for it was well-known that there were pirates along the coast. But Mr. Alston's letter to Colonel Burr describing the departure, best serves us here, as it sets aside some disputes:

Portrait from the Nag's Head
Supposed to be Theodosia Burr Alston

Aaron Burr's Watch with his Wife's Portrait

"I parted with our Theo near the bar at noon on Thursday, the last day of December. The wind was moderate and fair. She was in the pilot-built schooner, Patriot. Captain Overstocks, with an extra New York pilot, coon, as sailing master. This vessel, the same which had been sent by the government last summer in pursuit of Commodore Rodger's Squadron, had been selected as one, from her reputed experience and swiftness in sailing, would insure a passage of not more than five or six days. From that moment, I have heard nothing of the schooner nor my wife."

So the gallant ship sailed from harbor on the coast of South Carolina at noon on December 31, 1812, and was never heard of again. That night a terrific storm visited the coast, but it does not seem that there was any undue uneasiness until the time came for her arrival. Perhaps, no other two men's hearts were ever more centered in their love of one woman than were the hearts of this father and husband, who kept up a correspondence all the while. When two weeks past and no tidings came, Mr. Alston, on January 15, 1813, penned Theo a letter, which was filled with apprehension. This was followed by another distracted one, four days later. It read: "Tomorrow will be three weeks since our separation, and yet not one line. Gracious God! for what am I reserved?"

Mr. Alston, in his despair, at this same time, wrote his distracted father-in-law:

"To-morrow will be three weeks since in obedience to your wishes, Theodosia left me . . . My mind is tortured . . . Gracious God! is my wife too, taken from me? I do not know why I write, but I feel that I am miserable . . ." Then again when a month has gone by: "But Thirty days are decisive . . . My wife is either captured or lost!" Another letter in February continues Mr. Alston's cry of despair:

"My boy!—my wife!—gone both! This is the end of all the hopes we have formed. You may well observe that you feel severed from the human race. She was the last tie that bound us to the species. What have we left?—You knew those we loved. Here none knew them; none valued them as they deserved. The talents of my boy—made him regretted by the pride of my family; but though certain of the loss of my not less admirable wife, they seem to consider it like the loss of an ordinary woman . . . The man who has been deemed worthy of the heart of Theodosia Burr, and who has felt what it is to be blest with such a woman's love, will never forget his elevation."

Later Mr. Alston writes his father-in-law of the second shock that he received, after his double bereavement, when he visited The Oaks and saw the playthings of his child scattered about, and the belongings of his wife, as she had left them. And he thus continues:

"I visited the grave of my boy. The little plans that we had all three formed rushed upon my memory. Where now was the boy? the mother I cherished with so much pride. I felt like the very spirit of desolation. If it had not been for a kind of stupefaction, and confusion of mind which followed, God knows how I should have borne it. Oh! my friend, if there be such a thing as the sublime of misery, it is for us that it has been reserved.

"You are the only person in the world with whom I can converse on this subject; for you are the only person whose feelings can have any community with mine. You know those we loved."

These letters give one a glimpse into the despair of those weary days and weeks of waiting, which lengthened into months and finally, into years. All sorts of rumors were afloat as to the fate of the hapless vessel and its precious human freight, but the supposition that she had foundered off Cape Hatteras seemed to prevail. But long after all others had given up hope, a small figure might have been seen at the New York harbor peering far down the bay; as if trying to catch the glimpse of a sail or some rescuing vessel; but Colonel Burr finally gave up that she was dead. He knew that nothing could keep her silent toward him were she alive. This was the cruelest blow of his entire life—the climax of his sorrow. But the world knew little of his agony. In his grief, he declared that he felt as if he were severed from the entire human race. He finally rose above it until the light came to his countenance once more, "but it was ever a subdued light."

7

At The Oaks

Colonel Burr realized that his son-in-law was still young and encouraged him to continue in politics, but the double blow that deprived him of child and wife plunged him into such a gulf of despair that it wasn't but a few years until they made him a grave beside the little mound at The Oaks. His brilliant career, which has been surpassed by few young men in history of his years, seemed to end here. He had lost his inspiration, life no longer had any charm for him. He died of a broken heart on September 10, 1816, before he had reached his meridian. And he rests at The Oaks in All Saints Parish, Georgetown, South Carolina under the following epitaph, with a long tribute, besides, omitted:

"Sacred to the Memory
of
Joseph and Theo B. Alston
and of their son
A. B. A.
This last died June 30, 1812
at the age of ten years
and his remains are interred here.

"The disconsolate mother
perished a few months after at sea
And on the 10th of September, 1816
the father died
when little over thirty-seven years of age
whose remains rest with the son."

In his will, Mr. Alston left to Colonel Burr all demands against him, and Theodosia's entire belongings, including the trunk, which he could never bear to open, and which gave up her letter to him, written when she thought she was dying. His brother, William Alston, communicated the news of his death to Colonel Burr.

The Oaks, like many another old Southern plantation, suffered ravages during the war between the states, and finally passed from the hands of the Alstons, with the reservation of the burial ground and some volumes of the famous library; the mansion with its wonderful traditions was burned many years ago. But the story that hangs about the plantation will make its place secure in our history for all time. Such joy, promise, love, and sorrow have seldom, if ever, been so blended into thirty brief years of any life as that of the beautiful Theodosia Burr. For brilliancy, goodness, and charm, she had no peers among the women of her time, and none have since displaced her in American history. Her pathetic story has no equal in feminine annals, and it proves once again that "Truth is stranger than fiction, and far more appealing to the heart."

Mr. Alston, unlike his father-in-law, was not a favorite with the gentler sex, and some very uncomplimentary feminine estimates of him are left to us. Mrs. Blennerhassett has already spoken, and another comes from the lovely Nelly Custis in a letter to Mrs. Pinckney, 1801, in which she is speaking of a fashionable dance at

Williamsburg, which must have been during the honeymoon of Theodosia Burr:

"Colonel Burr, his daughter, and her husband were
there. Mrs. Alston is a very sweet, little woman, very
engaging and pretty—but her husband is the most
intolerable mortal I ever beheld. I cannot enough con-
gratulate dear Eliza [meaning her sister] on escaping a
union with him. I think he is more calculated to break
a wife's heart than any other person I have ever seen."
She admits in her comment that he has good sense, but
"it is securely locked in the recesses of his brain." But
despite the opinions of these fair onlookers, Joseph
Alston must have possessed qualities of manhood not
discernible to the casual observer, to have won and held
the adoration of such a woman as Theodosia Burr. Her
letters disclose the high standard that she has set for
him—not as a husband, alone, but as a father, and he
must have in some measure at least, attained to it; for
such adoration is seldom manifested by woman.

*Author's Note—According to the South Carolina Historical
Society, Joseph Alston, who served as governor of the State,
1812-1814, had been inaugurated but a few days when Theodosia started on this fatal journey; so she never presided as first
lady of the state.*

8

The End of the Trail

Colonel Burr lived on despite the cruelty of Fate, but life seemed to be one continuous struggle as the weight of years fell upon him. He had friends who were true, and he found comfort in their companionship, but he was truly a martyr to prejudice and persecution. As long as he was able to be about the streets, he was pointed out to the children as the "man who had killed Hamilton," but the child who gazed at him out of curiosity, was more often won by his kindly smile. A pen picture of him, silent and neglected, sitting alone in the parlors, gathering up crumbs of conversation which were interesting to him, is pathetic, indeed. One historian observes that he lived thirty-one years too long; that they could find nothing to inscribe upon his epitaph—nothing but tragedy and grief and suffering, and these they did not consider worth recording. Despite all that has been said to the contrary, there is overwhelming proof that he shared generously what he had to share—in that final day of reckoning there will be many entries to his credit side, without doubt. He did all he could to help those who suffered in his enterprise, but his means were powerless. He left his papers with his daughter when he was abroad, and his accounts for collection, but she could not collect them, and as they all went down with her at sea, there was nothing left to be done. In his hour of great need during the Richmond trial, Luther Martin had voluntarily stepped forward and rendered him all the service possible. It is said that Martin adored Theodosia, and on one occasion, Blennerhassett notes in his journal, "Luther Martin's admiration for Mrs. Alston is nearly as idolatrous as my own." However, when misfortune overtook Mr. Martin, 1822, Burr shared with him his own indifferent lodging, and cared for him till death relieved Martin's suffering. Many other such gentle deeds might be enumerated from written pages that are yet in existence.

His admiration for women and his innumerable intrigues with them would make a volume all its own, but this, too, has evidently been greatly exaggerated; for his respect for the good and the true in woman was marked to an unusual degree—as witnessed in his wife and his daughter. He seemed to have a peculiar fascination for the sex and was more often pursued by them. After all that has been said and written concerning his escapades, it sounds like some fairytale to hear him avow, "I have never deceived or made a false promise to a woman in my life." But the color of romance never lost its charm for him. When the sands of life were running low, and he was halting upon his staff at the age of seventy-seven, we find him taking the vow "till death do us part" with Madame Eliza Bowen Jumel, widow of Stephen Jumel, who was just the antithesis of the gentle Theodosia Prevost, but she had fortune. She is described as a person of low breeding, ill-temper, without education or character—one whom Burr had courted in his youth, and the bond did not hold. It was solemnized at the Jumel Mansion on July 1, 1833 by the same Reverend David Boggart, who had read the nuptial ceremony for Burr and Mrs. Prevost fifty-one years before, wanting a day, but how different the union. In a little more than a year, we find the bride of to-day instituting suit for divorce on the grounds of matrimonial offenses at divers times with other females, and to restrain her husband from wasting her property. But was it the irony of Fate that decreed that this divorce should be delayed until the very day that Madame Jumel was released from her vow "till death do us part?" for it was granted on the very day that Burr died.

Despite all his misfortune, Burr was not forsaken. Some Good Samaritan always seemed to be sent to provide for his needs. After his break with Mrs. Jumel when he was disabled by a third stroke of paralysis, he went to live in a boarding house which was kept in the old Jay mansion in New York by a good Scotch woman, whose father Burr had met while serving on opposite sides in the Revolution, and who befriended the "Exile" in his own home in Scotland, years after. This woman had learned from her father to look upon him as a wronged man, and when he could no longer receive clients, she administered to his needs, and the days passed pleasantly with old friends about him. He had a little money of his own, and his own servant to look after him; but this old mansion was to be torn down during the summer of 1836, and for the convenience of Judge Edwards, who looked after his business affairs, he was removed to the Winant Inn at Port Richmond on Staten Island. This was his final adieu to New York City, which had been the theater of so many events of his life. He was now old and feeble—just a mere wisp of his former self, and a few months later with the whispered word "Madame" he fell asleep.

One evening not long before the end, after the good woman had made him comfortable for the night before leaving, he took her by the hand and said, "May God, forever and forever, bless you, my last best friend. When the hour comes, I will look out in the better country for one bright spot for you, be sure."

He always had reverence for the Bible and had religious attention toward the last, but he never avowed religious conviction, in fact, he avoided the subject.

He often talked of his plans that had ended so fatally, and to his dying day affirmed that he had no thought of conquest* without actual declaration of war to legalize it. He once said, "I might as well have attempted to seize the moon and parcel it out." He closely followed the trend of events from his couch of pain; and when the independence of Texas was declared, he was old and an invalid. One morning a friend found him in a

Where Aaron Burr took his second marriage vow

Wiant Inn, where Burr died

frenzy of excitement; he had just read the account, and pointing to it exclaimed, "You see I was right! I was only thirty years too soon. What was treason in me thirty years ago, is patriotism now." Without doubt that had been the plan of his adventurous spirit, and jealousy and enmity born of his unusual brilliancy, had been his undoing.

They bore the remains back to Princeton and laid them at the feet of his father and grandfather with military honors. For a score of years he rested without epitaph, no monument was placed lest it meet with desecration. Finally a simple stone bearing this inscription, was erected:

> "Aaron Burr
> Born, February 6, 1756
> Died, September 14, 1836
> A Colonel in the Army of the Revolution
> Vice President of the U. S.
> From 1801-1805"

Whispers of illegitimate children are found in a number of his biographers, and there is little doubt that they existed. One of these is said to have provided this monument, as she was remembered in his will. Wandell and Minnegrode in their "Aaron Burr", say that Alfred Edwards had this cut in Brown's Marbleyard, New York, and placed it here.

9

Varied Comments on Burr

Aaron Burr is, without question, one of the most singular figures in our entire history; as well as one of the most brilliant and interesting. He, doubtless, has been portrayed in more lights by the moods, prejudices, and pens of men than any other one individual, and has been the victim of more abuse. While time and research are softening this censure and denunciation, we are still confronted by a medley of contradictions, which depict him all the way from devil to angel. Let us listen to a few of these biographical comments:

Jenkinson says, "Never in the history of the United States did so powerful a combination of rival politicians unite to break down a single man, as the one that arrayed itself against Burr. The conspiracy was too powerful. Burr was defeated and his political career, ended." He further says, "No man had truer friends; their devotion was almost unlimited, and in return he was true and faithful to them. Those who knew him best were his warmest and most trusting friends."

Henry Adams first speaks of this effort to ruin him, and says,

"It is beyond question that in the course of his long life, he had many intrigues with women, some of which (not many there is good reason to believe) were carried

to the point of criminality. The grosser form of licen-
tiousness, he utterly abhorred, such as the seduction of
innocence . . . Not every woman could attract him.
A woman of wit, vivacity, and grace, whether the
inhabitant of a mansion or a cottage . . . could
captivate him. Everything pertaining to the sex was
peculiarly interesting to him, even to the well-written
billet-doux."

Beveridge in his fine interpretation of the Burr
Conspiracy in his "Life of John Marshall", volume three,
in speaking of Burr as he walked the muddy streets of
Washington, at the close of his administration as vice
president, says in part:

"His fine ancestry counted for nothing with the
reigning politicians of either party. None of them cared
that he came of a family which, on both sides, was
among the worthiest in all the country. His superb
education went for naught. His brilliant services as one
of the youngest Revolutionary officers were no longer
considered—his heroism at Quebec; his resourcefulness
on Putnam's staff; his valor at Monmouth; his daring
and tireless efficiency at West Point, and on the Win-
chester Lines, were to these men, as if no such record
had ever been written."

Warren Wood, in "The Tragedy of the Deserted Isle,"
thinks: "His (Burr's) great lack was moral poise; had
he possessed the fine, ethical discrimination of Washington, he would have been invincible in any field. As it

was, he made Jefferson President; he taught the Democratic Party how to win; he graced the office of vice president, as none before or since; he inaugurated the movement that landed Andrew Jackson in the Presidential chair; he gave to the West an impetus that was felt to its farthest shore; he left to the world a rare example of cheerfulness and submission under all gradations of trial and misfortune."

Another says,

"Burr was a strange mixture of opposite natures combined. He was brilliant and studious; dignified and seductive. He was profligate in morals, selfish, artful; a master in dissimulation, treacherous, cold-hearted, subtle, intriguing, a scorner of all things noble and good. Thus he failed to gain public confidence and he fell headlong from his dizzy heights. There was no stability in his character to win public confidence, and it shrank in distrust from him." [Such a charge as this cannot be substantiated by fact.]

Another would have it thus:

"Burr had dreamed all too long of the wealth and splendor of the Montezumas to resign their captivating pleasure for the tamer scenes of a government in which he was daily becoming more unpopular, and which he now conceived viewed his actions with ungrateful suspicions. For years he had cherished the hope of investing himself with regal power of that ancient kingdom and transmitting its crown to his latest posterity. For the realization of this, he had sacrificed the comforts of home; traversed the states to the extremes of Florida, often traveling through the pathless wilderness—sometimes without shelter and occasionally without food, alluring to his standard men of every grace, prompted by every motive and action."

One Scribe observes: "Burr died as he lived without regard for good. His hoary hairs went down to the grave floating on the breeze of infamy." But this is not true—such a statement is wholly without foundation.

Parton, who thinks that politics was his undoing expresses it thus: "What happy years were these which Colonel Burr passed in the practice of law in New York before he was drawn into the vortex of politics. He speaks of his home life so replete with happiness, of his fatherly interest in his step-sons, who were students of law under him, and one of them, his amanuensis; and of "little Theodosia, a lovely, rosy-cheeked child, all grace and intelligence, the delight of the household," and pronounces him the happiest of men. He further says, "In these happy days there was no blot on his fair name; happy at home, honored abroad . . . It was 1801 when the tide really begun to turn with disastrous results."

More than one biographer is persuaded that the Richmond trial would never have been had it not been

* See what Blennerhassett papers tell, page 84.

for the "jealousy of Jefferson and the perfidy of Wilkinson."

Safford wrote:

"He [Burr] was arrested, tried, and acquitted, but his country refused to believe him innocent. Though stout old Truxton testified in his favor; Jackson had seen nothing wrong in his project, but had agreed to favor it, the popular voice has continued to regard him as a traitor whom accident alone prevented from dismembering the Union. That a man of sense and ability should entertain such a notion, relying for aid on associates whom he knew would countenance no treason, is a preposterous and insane proposition."

Henry Child Merwin would have it thus:

"When all the other witnesses have been heard let the two Theodosias be summoned, and especially that daughter who showed toward him an affectionate veneration unsurpassed by any recorded in history or romance. Such an advocate as Theodosia, the younger, must avail in some degree, even though the culprit were brought before the bar of Heaven itself."

We have already included much of this testimony of both wife and daughter, but acting upon the suggestion of Mr. Merwin, let us hear another bit from Theodosia, the younger:

"I witness your extraordinary fortitude with new wonder at every new misfortune. Often reflecting on this subject, you appear to me so superior, so elevated over all other men; I contemplate you with such strange a mixture of humility, admiration, reverence, love, and pride, that very little superstition would be necessary to make me worship you as a superior being, such enthusiasm does your character excite in me. When I afterwards revert to myself, how insignificant do my best qualities appear. My vanity would be greater if I had not been placed so near you; and yet my pride is our relationship. I had rather not live than not be the daughter of such a man."

Wandell in his "Aaron Burr" adds, "Perhaps it is the justification of his whole life that he should have been the father of such a daughter." This Author finds "a strain of insanity in the family" which may account for some of the madcap moments of Burr. When two such superior women, and these women wife and daughter, especially, unite in a verdict like this there must be something good in a man, notwithstanding outside estimate to the contrary. Women are not prone to idolize the cold, the cruel, the selfish, the debased as depicted in Burr. And may it not have been the innate tenderness, the superior intellect, the rare courtesy of manner, that made him the idol of the home, that had something to do with the secret of his power over his fellowmen in general? It has been said that a man's ideal of womanhood is a key to his inner self. If this be true, we must change our estimate of Aaron Burr when we behold that ideal in such a wife and daughter.

There is pathos in the story of Burr which is almost without parallel. In the multitude of accusations against him, none has yet been sustained. No one knows even at this late day that he ever entertained a thought of treason. The whole cruel verdict has been mere opinion, more often for want of knowledge, without fact to sustain it.

Walter Flavius McCaleb, who, according to Beveridge, "exploded the Burr Treason Myth" in his book, "The Aaron Burr Conspiracy," in 1903, came out in revised edition, 1936, with additional Prologue and Epilogue, which stand firmly to justice in this episode.

He recalls that in June, 1836, when Burr was thought to be dying, he was again asked in regard to his designs in separating the Union, and he replied, "No! I would as soon have thought of taking possession of the moon, and informing my friends that I intended to divide it among them."

McCaleb further speaks of "Burr's putting out to sea," and thus continues:

"Once at twilight, the writer of these lines stood at the foot of Burr's grave, and beside him was Woodrow Wilson, then president of Princeton. As we neared the place, he removed his hat—and so did I. Then with bowed heads, we stood for a moment in silence. Suddenly Wilson spoke—and how prophetic of his own fate—his voice was pitched very low—'How misunderstood——how maligned——!' " McCabe then continues:

"Why is it, indeed, that nearly always, the truly great souls come down to us misunderstood and broken in the gins of life!"

10

Richmond Hill, the Home of Burr

At the mention of Richmond Hill, we first think of it as the headquarters of the beloved Commander-in-Chief of the Continental forces, and see a youth with laurels, fresh from the battlefield of Quebec, joining him here; but let us turn the leaves of Time farther back to when it became Richmond Hill.

It seems that Trinity Church held a lease on these fair forest-clad hills in 1760 when Abraham Mortier, the paymaster for the Royal forces in the Colonies, obtained possession, and he crowned its highest point with a fine mansion, surrounded by spacious grounds, for the estate contained one hundred sixty acres, which he called Richmond Hill. Sixteen years later, 1776, when General Washington moved on to New York, he took up his headquarters here; and upon the arrival of Major Burr from Canada in May, he waited upon the Commander-in-Chief in this mansion. General Washington remained here until the retreat of the Continental Army to Harlem Heights when he withdrew to the Roger Morris home, later the Jumel Mansion, where the lovely Mary Philipse Morris had reigned as queen of the household. Little did young Burr dream when he first crossed this threshold on that fair May day with his heart beating high with promise, what love, joy, tragedy, and despair this old mansion held in store for him!

The British Officers later made it their headquarters, while they held possession of New York, and it was here that the conspiracy was hatched for the poisoning of General Washington, and other officers of the Continental Army, which was uncovered in time to prevent the tragedy.

In 1789 Mrs. Jephson was in possession, and at the assembling of the first Congress of the United States in New York, it became the home of Vice President John Adams, and Mrs. Adams was so delighted with her surroundings here, that we are now permitted to glimpse it through a description given to her sister, Mrs. Shaw on September 27, 1789, which reads in part:

"I write to you, my dear Sister, not from the banks of the Potomac, the Susquehanna or the Delaware, but from the peaceful borders of the Hudson—a situation where the hand of Nature has so lavishly displayed her beauties that she has left scarcely anything for her handmaiden, Art, to perform.

"The house in which we reside is situated upon a hill, the avenue to which is interspersed with forest trees, under which a shrubbery rather too luxuriant and wild has taken shelter, owing to its having been deprived by death some years since of its original proprietor, who kept it in perfect order. In front of the house, the noble Hudson rolls his majestic waves, bearing upon his bosom innumerable small vessels, which are constantly forwarding the rich products of the neighboring soil to the busy hand of a more extensive commerce. Beyond the Hudson rises to our view the fertile country of the Jerseys, covered with a golden harvest, and pouring forth plenty like the Cornucopia of Ceres. On the right hand an extensive plain presents us with a view of fields covered with verdure and pastures full of cattle. On the left, the city opens upon us, intercepted only by clumps of trees and some rising grounds, which serve to heighten the beauty of the scene, by appearing to conceal a part. In the background is a large flower garden, enclosed with a hedge, and some very handsome trees. On one side of it is a grove of pines and oaks fit for contemplation.

> '*In this path*
> *How long so e'er the wanderer*
> *roves, each step*
> *Shall wake fresh beauties!*
> *each last point present*
> *A different picture, new, and yet*
> *the same.*'

"If my days of fancy and romance were not past, I could here find an ample field for indulgence. Yet amidst these delightful scenes of Nature my heart pants for the society of my dear relatives and friends."

After such a description, it is small wonder that it made its appeal to Burr, who obtained possession, perhaps, near the year 1793; and the old mansion added not a few colorful pages to its historical, social, and romantic calendar, while the Burrs lived here, as well as some of its most somber pages; for it was here that Mrs. Burr died, and it was the tragedy of Weehawken that closed its doors against Burr forever. It was sacrificed for debt, and from that hour, its interest waned.

John Jacob Astor purchased the estate, all but the mansion and a few acres about it, later; and soon after this transaction, the mansion was sold for twenty-five thousand dollars. Then neglect, solitude, and decay came to these cherished walls; the city moved nearer; the population spread its wings; and the beautiful site was finally lowered from its ideal heights to one hundred feet below, transforming it into a commonplace, every day sort of corner house on the southwest of Charlton and Verick Streets. A circus occupied it in 1819; then in turn it played the role of public house, theater, and at length became Tivoli Gardens. By and by Richmond Hill Theater attracted the westside and great stage favorites appeared before its footlights, but the populace moved on, and the gentility of Richmond Hill was replaced by the shabby and uninviting, and its fame sank into oblivion, like that of its Master.

11

What Later Years Have Disclosed

Long years had passed, since the reunion of the Burr Family on the other side, before any light was thrown on the mystery that enshrouded the disappearance of Theodosia Burr; as the theory concerning the foundering of the gallant ship had been generally accepted, despite the many colorful rumors. But by and by stories of a more credible nature, began to come. Deathbed confessions of seamen and condemned criminals to be heeded. In accord with these, "A schooner-built pilot boat," which had been boarded by the wreckers, who were so famous in that war along the coast, drifted ashore at Kitty Hawk. One story was to the effect that the boat had been abandoned; that apparel belonging to a lady of refinement was scattered about the cabin, and that a beautiful, feminine portrait was taken ashore. A number of accounts agreed that such a vessel as the Patriot was driven ashore at Kitty Hawk in a violent storm, which shattered the British Fleet off Cape Hatteras, at this time. It has been since authenticated, too, that the remains of a young woman of evident refinement drifted ashore at Cape Charles, Virginia, early in the year, 1813, and were buried on the farm of the man who picked them up. But more than a century has passed and that grave still holds its secret.

The Philadelphia Times of February 20, 1880, contained the story of the discovery of a beautiful portrait in a cottage at Nag's Head, some fifty miles north of Cape Hatteras, which was occupied by an old woman, who had been the wife of one of the noted wreckers in those days, and this story has often been repeated since then with verifications and additions, by those who have investigated it.

However, Dr. W. C. Pool, of Elizabeth, North Carolina, was spending the summer with his family, at Nag's Head, when he was called to see the old woman occupant of this cottage professionally. There among these unwholesome surroundings, he saw the beautiful portrait of a young woman, which deeply impressed him, but he seemed restrained from asking about it. One day he was accompanied by his little daughter, who was so drawn toward the portrait that the old lady gave it to her. Reluctantly the woman disclosed the following information: When this pilot boat drifted ashore at Kitty Hawk, her husband, Mr. Tilton, then her sweetheart, went on board with the wreckers, and among other things belonging to a woman in this deserted cabin, was this portrait. The breakfast table had not been molested, though it was spread, which suggested the morning hour when the blow fell. Trunks had been forced open, silken dresses, and other feminine apparel lay scattered about with the picture. While there were no visible signs of violence, it was evident that those on board had been compelled to walk the plank. Mr. Tilton came in for his share of the spoils, and this portrait, two dresses, and a shell were his portion. The hesitating manner in which the recital was given left Dr. Pool to think that much had been omitted. Dr. Pool's daughter verified this story in after years.

Claude Burr Todd, the author of the "True Aaron Burr" being in reach of Dr. Pool's home, 1889, called to see the portrait, and was impressed with its strong resemblance to others of the beautiful woman. He described it as an oil painting on wood with gilt frame about twenty inches in length, corresponding in art with the first decade of the century. He went to Nag's Head* for an interview with the sons of the woman; they disclaimed any knowledge of the story, but an elder sister, at Roanoke, recalled the portrait and a chest of drawers that her mother had told her of in childhood, which had floated to shore, but she had not heard about the gowns.

One of the pirate's stories is told on the credit of M. L. Stone, whose father, Colonel William L. Stone, heard the deathbed confession in the Toombs in Alabama by one who was known as "Babe" in this prison. According to Babe's confession, all the crew and passengers had been destroyed, except Mrs. Alston, and no one seemed willing to take her life; as she had not resisted or fought; and when they drew lots as to who should do this deed, the lot fell on him. He had not

*See Nag's Head Portrait, from Pidgin's "Theodosia Burr," page 152.

the courage, but laid a plank along the edge of the ship and made her walk it until it tilted her into the water. He asked that this story be made public after he was dead, but his family objected.

Another pirate, who died in an alms house in the West, in the early Fifties made a confession, which was published twenty years later by Stella E. P. Drake of Sturgis, Missouri, who claimed to be the pirate who made Mrs. Alston walk the plank, and this is his story: When she was told that she must walk the plank into the sea, she asked for a few moments; then came forth beautifully gowned in white—the loveliest woman that he had ever seen. Calmly she stepped upon that fatal plank, with her eyes raised to heaven and her hands crossed serenely upon her bosom, and slowly and firmly, she walked into the ocean. While these stories are not unreasonable, we can but take them for what they are worth with the attendant doubt.

Pidgin, in his epilogue of the Story of Burr, which is supposed to be fiction, but which has much fact in the background, relates the tale of the bottle, which was picked up off the coast of Iceland by a fisherman, and which contained two letters—one addressed to Aaron Burr and the other to Joseph Alston, sealed with the letter B. This bottle is also supposed to have included a manuscript, disclosing the full account of the ill-fated Patriot from the time she left port to the night Theodosia accompanied Captain Thaddeus Stevens she knew not whither. It is further disclosed in this narrative that Captain Stevens fell into the hands of Captain Hamilton, and the beautiful woman was accidentally shot. According to Pidgin's sequel to the manuscript story, she lingered until the following morning, and was buried at sea, as there was nothing to lead to her identity. "My father" in French, being the only words she uttered.

This is a clever piece of fiction woven about the final hours of the unfortunate woman; and the introduction of the name Hamilton as the destroyer of this idol of Colonel Burr's heart, makes it only the more forcibly dramatic.

Pidgin later wrote an authentic story of Theodosia Burr in which he admits that he "wanders from historical fact into the realm of the fanciful" when he repines over what might have been had Theodosia been the beloved wife of Washington Irving and the mistress of Sunnyside instead of The Oaks, as he is sure she should have been. He pictures her in the protecting love of husband and father, perhaps, spared from many of the sorrows that overtook her. Had this been her happy fate, he thinks it possible that the wrangle with Jefferson, the deadly affair at Weehawken, the mystery of the Ohio River Island, and the awful tragedy at sea might have been averted. He, too, permits himself to be carried further into the realm of imagination when he ventures to associate the "Mysterious Female Stranger" of Alexandria with Theodosia Burr, but such unsolved mysteries are far-reaching in their surmises more often. True, it is possible that the beautiful woman could have been carried into captivity, and detained against her wishes; but it is hardly probable that any captor who knew her identity would have dared to even think of selecting Alexandria as a place of concealment for a woman so well-known; and it would be a poor historian indeed, that would attempt to associate the name of Joseph Alston with the Alexandria incident. For Joseph Alston had been resting at the Oaks for more than a month when this interesting Female Stranger, died at the Gadsby Hotel at Alexandria on October 14, 1816. She and her husband stepped from a ship that was just in from the West Indies, a few weeks before, and registered at this tavern. She was very ill of fever and lingered until death relieved her. Her husband seemed much devoted to her, and laid her at rest at Alexandria beneath a unique epitaph which disclosed nothing as to her identity, and then stole away as quietly as he had come. Years after a citizen of Alexandria saw this same Stranger in Sing Sing Prison in New York, but he had so many aliases that even the prison authorities did not know his name, though he was an Englishman of culture and education. See Mrs. Powell's "History of Old Alexandria," for complete story.

Such mysteries seem unsolvable, and we must leave this one until all mysteries are revealed.

12

The Curtain Drops

Was it the irony of Fate that brought tragedy into the lives of all who played a part in the drama that centered about the once beautiful Island? However, it is another evidence that "truth is stranger than fiction," and far more impressive. It is an unsolved mystery, since nothing was ever sustained against any of them, and few, if any, except Wilkinson, seemed conscious of wrong-doing. But the fact remains that darkness and despair was the "cup" of each and everyone until death veiled them from human sight.

As we already know Harman Blennerhassett and his wife wandered and suffered until they found graves divided by the tossing deep; their children, blighted by dissipation, were a sad disappointment, and their descendants were entirely wiped out early in the second generation.

Wilkinson was court-martialed and dismissed from the Army, though the charges were not sustained; and ruined in reputation and fortune, he withdrew to Mexico where he died on December 28, 1825, near the city that must have been a constant reminder of his perfidy.

Burr "blazed like a meteor across the sky of American history," only to have his light go out in despair. Bereft of all he held dear he lived on and on after every hope had perished. Gamp, the little grandson, about whom so many fond hopes were entwined, vanished from sight one beautiful June day. His idolized daughter sailed away never to return. Her husband died of a broken heart before he had reached the meridian of life.

It is one of the most impressive pictures in our American history. And it is one that should bespeak a broader charity for the short-comings of our fellowman; and the witholding of harsh judgment until there is some evidence to base it upon.

Theodosia Burr and Margaret Blennerhassett were equally favored with the advantages of birth, wealth, and education. Everything bespoke promise and happiness. None could have believed that such awful night was in store for the idolized Theodosia; but the fate of Margaret Blennerhassett was worse. It is another impressive reminder of the vanity, the uncertainty of all human hopes.

Thus the curtain falls upon one of the most absorbing dramas in American History. Let us trust if it rises again, that the new Blennerhassett may be firmly grounded upon the rock of truth and justice; that no falsity may enter this new domain against these actors of other years, whose shades can never be divorced from the spot.

The End

Note—The appendix is included in the cloth-bound edition only.

INDEX

Miller, Robert, obtains charge of the Island under writ of, 108.
Mills, John, host to Burr, 45.

N

Neale, George II, 5; will of, 109.
George, the elder, will of, 109, 111; Agnes R., 109, 110; Sarah, Pocahontas, and Lucy, 111.
Neville, Morgan, affidavit, 97.
Nelson, Herron & Co., 106.

O

Osmen, Colonel's Mount awaits Burr, 41.

P

Perkins, Colonel Nicholas, suspicions stranger, 42-46; follows to Fort Stoddart, 43, 44, 45, 47, 48.
Phelps, Colonel, 25.
Plumer, Senator, doubts Burr's guilt, 40.
Putnam, David, 4, 108; Aaron Waldo, 114.

Q

Queen of the Realm, 15.

R

Randolph, John, foreman of jury, 52; comment on Wilkinson, 55.
Robinson, William, Junior, 97.

S

Safford, W. H., author of Blennerhassett Island, and Papers, 83, 111.
Shaw, Gabriel, at Island, 17.
Smith, Israel, 31.

T

Tiffin, Governor of Ohio, authorizes call of Militia, 30.
Tupper, General Edward, 32, 59.
Tyler, Comfort, 31, 33, 39, 95.

U

Utretch, Long Island, letter from Blennerhassett to nephew, on landing, 10.

V

Vinty, Lord buys Blennerhassett Estate in Ireland, 9.

W

Washington, Col. George, 106.
Wheatley R., attorney for Blennerhassetts, 100.
Wickham, 61.
Williams, Governor of Miss. manifests hostility to Burr, 38.
Wilkinson, General, meets Burr at Fort Massac, 19; "turns patriot" detains bearer of cipher letter, dispatches, messenger to Washington, excites the President, 26-28; testifies in trial, and admits he altered cipher letter, 53; pronounced a villain, 55; perjured, 63.
Wirt, William, description of Island, 13; at the bar, 61; Blennerhassett's Journal comment on Wirt, 69.
Woodbridge, Dudley, business partner of Blennerhassett, 23; witness in trial, 58; goes bond for Blennerhassett, 69;

PART II
A

Alston, Joseph, pleads his own

cause as suitor, and the marriage takes place, 133-134; letter to Burr concerning Theodosia's departure at sea, 152-153; letters of despair, 154-5; visits The Oaks, and sees playthings, 154-5; dies of broken heart and rests at The Oaks, 156; letter addressed to him, 178, 180.

Alston, Family, founders of The Oaks, 135; Nellie Custis's comment on Joseph Alston, 158.

Ashe, General; Mary Ashe, 135.

B

Burr, Aaron, parentage and ancestry; his father one of the founders of Princeton, and his marriage to Esther Edwards; birth of little Aaron, and mother's journal description of him; death of his parents and grandparents; adoption by his uncle; runs away to sea, 121-125; Sallie Burr married Tappan Reeve, 126; in the expedition to Canada, 126-7; marriage to Mrs. Prevost, and Theodosia born, 128-30; death of Mrs. Burr, 131; Theodosia and Natalie Hostesses at Richmond Hill, and Natalie's marriage, 132; Theodosia's marriage, 134; rivalry with Hamilton and duel, 139-141; Theodosia's grief and letter to her husband when she thought death near, 141-5;

in exile, 146; watch for Little Gamp, 148-9; back to the Homeland, 149; death of Little Gamp, and distracted letters of parents, 150; Theodosia lost at Sea, and her husband's letters of despair, 153-5; pen picture of Burr in pathos, 159; Luther Martin's adoration for Theodosia, 160; marriage to Madame Jumel 160; death and burial, 163. Comments by varied authors, Jenkinson, and Henry Adams, 164-170, McCaleb, 170.

E

Edwards, Rev. Jonathan, 121, 123; Timothy and Mrs. Sarah, 124.

J

Jumel, Madame, 160, 161.

R

Richmond Hill, the home of Burr; headquarters of General Washington, 171; home of Vice President and Mrs. John Adams, and Mrs. Adam's description of it, 172-4.

S

Stories of Pirates concerning tragedy of Theodosia Burr, 175-180. Female Stranger at Alexandria, 180.

Appendix

—A—
Outstanding Works on Burr-Blennerhassett

—B—
Deposition of Alexander Henderson

—C—
Extracts from Blennerhassett's Brief in Court

—D—
Text of Burr's Cipher Letter to Wilkinson

—E—
Names of Grand Jurors in Burr Trial

A

Outstanding works on Burr-Blennerhassett

As stated in the preface, this book is based upon the new disclosure of Blennerhassett Papers placed in the Manuscript Department of the Library of Congress, 1921, by Therese Blennerhassett Adams—especially part one. But our research in general was in the Library of Congress where everything under copyright is available, and much besides; so it would be impossible to enumerate the scope of this research, neither would it be profitable, as the careful historian will not cite works that he, himself, has found wholly untrustworthy. But in reply to the many questions that have confronted us, and for the benefit of those who are seeking authentic works on this episode, we append this list:

"The Burr Trials," or stenographic court proceedings in two volumes, which are now found in our West Virginia State Library as well as in the Library of Congress.

"The Private Journal of Aaron Burr," reprinted from the Bixby Manuscripts.

"The Matthew Livingston Davis Memoirs of Aaron Burr," two volumes, 1838, authorized biography, which contains selections of Burr's Letters, "Correspondence of Burr with his Daughter, Theodosia," 1929, Covici-Friede, New York, edited with preface by Mark Van Doren.

Albert James Pickett's "History of Alabama," which contains the generally accepted story of Burr's capture and transportation to Richmond.

"Life and Times of Aaron Burr, 1858," by James Parton, who tells Pickett's Story, with additional incidents. While Parton is considered a bit inaccurate at times, perhaps, no other historian writes more interestingly or intimately of the life of Burr in its various phases. For instance, Chapter 33, "Anecdotes and Reminiscences of his later years"; Chapter 34, "His Relations with Women"; Chapter 35, "His Second Marriage"; Chapter 36, "His Last Years and Hours."

James Parton's "Life of Andrew Jackson," 1861, in three volumes, imparts much information concerning Burr and his colonization idea. Parton says in this, "The real prosecutor of Burr throughout this business, was Thomas Jefferson, President of the United States, who was made president by Aaron Burr's tact and vigilance, and who was able to wield against Aaron Burr the power and resources of the United States." See also McCaleb.

James Wilkinson's "Memoirs of My Own Times," three volumes, 1816.

"Private Correspondence of Henry Clay," edited by Calvin Colton, in which Clay gives the following description of the demonstration in the Kentucky Courthouse when Burr was arraigned:

"When the grand jury returned the bill of indictment not true, a scene was presented in the court room, which I had never before witnessed in Kentucky. There were shouts of applause from an audience, not one of whom . . . would have hesitated to level a rifle against Colonel Burr, if he had believed that he aimed to dismember the Union." See also Beveridge in "Life of John Marshall," volume 3, footnote, page 319.

A publication known as the *Palladium* in Kentucky, under date of November 13, 1806, made this comment: "Colonel Burr has throughout this business conducted himself with the calmness, moderation, and firmness, which have characterized him through life. He evinced an earnest desire for a full and speedy investigation—free from irritation or emotion, he excited the strongest sensation of respect and friendship in the breast of every impartial person present." See McCaleb, page 179.

"The Aaron Burr Conspiracy," by Professor Walter Flavius McCaleb, 1903, is classed as one of the best yet written upon this episode. Beveridge in his "Life of John Marshall," volume 3, footnote, page 289, classes Jenkinson's "Life of Aaron Burr" as the most trustworthy account until the appearance of McCaleb's book. McCaleb revised his book by additional preface, prologue and epilogue, in 1936; it came from the press about the time this little volume appeared on the horizon; and the new volume is now accessible in the Parkersburg Public Library, as well as in the State Library, and while we had not seen this edition until now, it runs almost parallel in its revision with our research.

Albert J. Beveridge, in his "Life of John Marshall," four volumes, 1916-1918, volume 3, is considered without peer in the interpretation of this episode, because it is a summary of the best authorities of that time, with the court trial behind it.

Those of us who have had access to these books in the background—many of which are now out of print—realize the value of Beveridge's contribution, which is generally found in libraries today.

See quotations from Burr authors in "Varied Comments on Burr" in this volume, pages 164-170.

"Journal of Esther Edwards Burr," mother of Aaron Burr, Library of Congress.

"Life and Letters of Washington Irving," four volumes, 1869.

Safford's "Life of Blennerhassett," 1850, which needs revising today. "The Blennerhassett Papers," edited by Safford, 1859.

But the later Blennerhassett Papers shed much new light on the whole affair. See pages 84-96, of this volume.

B

Deposition of Alexander Henderson
in the
Burr-Blennerhassett Episode of 1806

"About the first of September, 1806, I received a letter from Mr. Blennerhassett, informing me that with Mrs. Blennerhassett, he meant to visit my family. In the course of a few days, he came on the day appointed, accompanied by my brother, John. After taking some refreshments, Mr. Blennerhassett began a conversation about the severance of the Union; talked of the advantage that would be to the Western people to have a government of their own, saying that instead of three million of dollars which we paid towards the support of the present government at this time, with one hundred thousand dollars, we might support a government of our own. He then mentioned Col. Burr, as a man of brilliant talents, as well as great goodness of heart or words to that effect; that he had advanced the fortunes of hundreds without at all benefitting his own, and mentioned an instance—The Manhattan Company.

"This conversation took place, I think, before dinner. After we had dined, a walk in my meadow was proposed, during which Mr. Blennerhassett, saying that he had great confidence in my brother and myself, and from being assured that it was not misplaced, proceeded to inform us that under the auspices of Col. Burr, separation of the Union was contemplated; that it was not as yet ascertained whether the Allegheny, or what would be the particular line of division; that New Orleans was to be secured; the banks and the military stores in that country, and a fine patch of French Artillery, which was at or near New Orleans, and that country revolutionized in the course of nine months. That by means of these, and having possession of the mouth of the Mississippi, we could not long remain neutral, but should be compelled to take an active part for or against. In order to induce us to join, Mr. Blennerhassett told us that he had embarked in the plan; that the officers of the army and navy, that the leading characters throughout the Union were engaged, and particularly mentioned Gen. Eaton and Mr. John Graham, with the latter of whom I had been long and intimately acquainted. He said, as well as I remember, that Robert Harper was known to it, and that Mr. Alston was enamored (?) of the scheme.

"During the conversation many questions were asked, among which my brother asked Mr. Blennerhassett what kind of government was proposed in lieu of the present. The answer was that that was not as yet ascertained, but that it was expected a more energetic one. My brother then asked if any foreign power was concerned in it. Mr. Blennerhassett said there was not. Having heard that the leading characters throughout the Union were engaged, my brother asked if Mr. J. Randolph was acquainted with the scheme. The answer by Mr. Blennerhassett was that he believed not.

"Mr. and Mrs. Blennerhassett remained with us that night, and the next day until after an early dinner, during which time a deal of conversation passed, principally on the aforementioned subject. Among other things, he said that Col. Burr intended to tie the President neck and heels; and that with three pieces of artillery and 300-sharpshooters, he could defend any pass of the Alleghenies. Mr. Blennerhassett read us the manuscript . . . [Undecipherable] in the course of the afternoon, and left us for Marietta, whither, he said, he must go in order to attend to the publication.

"With reluctance, I consented that my son should go with Mrs. Blennerhassett to the Island, to stay two or three weeks with her children.

"Three or four days after their departure, I sent for the boy, drew from Mr. Blennerhassett the second letter, which hinted at the advantages that would arise to those who should take an early and active part. About the first of October, my brother and myself went to the mouth of the Kanawha to let Mr. Blennerhassett know that we had come to a full, decided determination to take an open and active part against his measure. But finding that he had gone to Kentucky to Mr. Alston, we sent that message to him. Then proposed a meeting of the citizens of Wood County, the consequences of which were the resolutions and military preparations that were afterwards so much the subject of animadversion.

"On the 20th of November, I received a letter from Mr. Graham, earnestly requesting an interview with him at the mouth of Kanawha. On the 22d, I met him there, and finding that he was not only not concerned in, but on the contrary was authorized to take such measures as he should think most proper for defeating any scheme hostile to the peace and honor of our country. And, conceiving myself, independent of motives of patriotism, every way justified in communicating with him, I therefore did give him the information, the substance of which is contained in this deposition."*

---

*This is an exact copy of the original deposition of Alexander Henderson, as given in the Burr Trial. It is now in the hands of his grandson, Jock B. Henderson, of Williamstown, who furnished it to us. The manuscript referred to is evidently the one signed "Querist" which has already been included in an earlier chapter.

C

Extracts from Blennerhassett's Brief in Court

Sections 1 and 2—Deal with his meeting of Burr, and his first letter to Burr, which has been included in this book, pages 20-21.

Section 3—Burr's second visit to the Island, as told in text of book.

Section 4—First trip to Marietta to see D. Woodbridge about boats, as told in text of book.

Sections 5, 6, 7, 8—Sentiments of People in Orleans and Mississippi and separation question, and Burr's reticence to explain, etc. And Blennerhassett's doubt of the sufficiency of Colonel Burr's credit in New York to meet the demands for boats and provisions, which he, himself, would indemnify for the company in case of failure on Burr's part.

Section 9—deals with the "Querist" Articles and the design of publishing them, and reads as follows:

"Some time in the month of August or September, 1806, your client, reflecting on the information and views disclosed to him [Blennerhassett], as a foresaid, by Colonel Burr, conceived the design of publishing in the Ohio Gazette, a short series of essays, calling the attention of the people of the Western Country to a subject that might engage their interests. Three or four numbers of these papers were published, exhibiting succinctly a general and relative view in a political aspect of the Union and the Western Country; and setting forth motives of right expediency which should induce the country west of the mountains to seek separation from the Atlantic States in a peaceable and constitutional manner; if they should adopt the sentiments of the writer, who took the signature of "Querist."*

---

*See text of book in earlier chapter for "Querist," page 24.

"The Author in making this essay on the public mind in that quarter, had no view of aggrandizement for himself, or of a political establishment for Colonel Burr in the Western Company, who [Burr] assured him he neither desired nor would accept anything within the United States. Your client was actuated to make the publication by two motives, namely, to prepare the country by a proper direction of its interests and energies for a crisis sooner or later approaching them—not from the views or operations of Colonel Burr, but from the state of things on the Mississippi; at which their espousal of an eastern or western ascendancy would determine their future prosperity, and to divert public attention from scrutiny into contingent plans or operations against Spain, which, while kept secret, government would not disapprove; but when exposed, it would be obliged to frustrate, as it had done in New York in the case of Ogden & Smith."

Section 10—"With these views, the Prisoner pledged his honor to Fairlamb, the printer of the Gazette, that he would publish nothing that would subject him to legal penalty, and the Prisoner would avow himself the author whenever it might become necessary to exonerate the printer from any responsibility. In the same spirit and for the same purposes, communicated his design, and read the manuscript of one of the first numbers to John & Alexander Henderson, who solemnly pledged their joint honors to the Prisoner, under the sanction of hospitality in the house of said Alexander, never to disclose the name of the author of the communication he then made them, to the purport and intent that are set forth in the fifth and ninth articles."

Sections 11, 12, 13—Include Blennerhassett's visit to Kentucky to witness Burr's growing popularity; his call home by the alarm of Mrs. Blennerhassett and the movements of the Militia, etc., which has all been told in the text of the book.

Section 14—Continues with the alarm on the Island upon his return, and touches on the ill-treatment from the Hendersons, and the purchase of lands; of General Jackson's interest in the movement, etc. He tells of the conversation with Col. Phelps in regard to the movement in which he [Colonel Phelps] saw no wrong; and he further speaks of making some propositions to Colonel Phelps in regard to renting the Island to Thomas Creel, the son-in-law of Colonel Phelps.

Sections 15, 16, 17—deal with the threatening conditions about the Island, preparations for flight, etc., already familiar.

Sections 18 and 19—consist of unimportant comments on things already familiar.

Sections 20 and 21—conclude the articles of the brief. Prefatory in these, Blennerhassett waxes sarcastic in regard to the Hendersons and their home which he calls Beech Park, and continues: "Arrived at the Temple erected to Honor and Hospitality in Beech Park, on the banks of the Little Kanawha, he is received in the vestibule by John & Alexander Henderson, the consecrated ministers of those divinities. A libation is now ordained to ancient friendship, and the household gods. Another is next proposed to the tutelary deities of the place, 'Hold!' cries the envoy of suspicion, 'the rites of Honour and Hospitality may be administered by their votaries in these sequestered wilds. But I will never participate in such mummery before that altar on which you have sacrificed to treason and to Burr.' His brother priests are now dismayed and almost petrified. 'Yes!' continued the ambassador, 'the safety of the State demands a greater sacrifice to liberty. Now purge ye of the charge committed to your keeping of all the crimes intended to be perpetuated against your country.' In vain the distracted brothers declare, 'No secrets of a dangerous nature were intrusted to their sanctum—they were innocent and submitted also by him, who trusted them, to sanction in the breast

of an aged parent.' Say you parent, innocent secrets, and submitted for sanction to the breast of a parent? Why not disclose
them to the parent of the State? I am his minister and will take
charge of them!"

Section 21—continues rather apologetically thus:

"Your client hopes the last paragraph may not displease by
its length or obscurity. The style he has there fallen into insen-
sibly suggested and protracted by his reflections on the intelligence
he received from Morgan Neville, Esquire, that it cost Mr.
Secretary Graham no little labor to work the Hendersons up
to break the seal of that Honour and Hospitality which the
prisoner imagined they would preserve inviolable, when he
made confidential communication to them, and through them
to their father, to the effect set forth in the fifth and ninth Articles"
—Wallace's "Blennerhassett." See full text of brief in Safford's
"Life of Blennerhassett," 1850; in Burr Trials, etc. Graham
does not occupy an enviable position in this episode; as his
accounts are classed at variance. See McCaleb, chapter 9, page
242, for this phase of the event; also "Tiffin's Message," 244-45.
Plot, McCaleb, 164.

There seems to have been no variations in the testimonies of
the Hendersons and Blennerhassett, except their viewpoints of
the movements.

D

Text, as generally accepted, of the Cipher Letter of
Aaron Burr to James Wilkinson, dated July 29, 1806*

"Your letter, postmarked thirteenth of May, is received. At
length I have obtained funds, and have actually commenced.
The Eastern detachments, from different points and under different pretences, will rendezvous on the Ohio first of November.
Everything internal and external favors our views. Naval protection of England is secured. Truxtun is going to Jamaica to
arrange with the Admiral on that Station. It will meet us at
the Mississippi. England, a navy of the United States, are
ready to join, and final orders are given to my friends and
followers. It will be a host of choice spirits. Wilkinson shall be
second to Burr only; Wilkinson shall dictate the rank and pro-
motion of his officers. Burr will proceed westward first August,
never to return. With him goes his daughter; her husband will
follow in October with a corps of worthies. Send forthwith an
intelligent and confidential friend with whom Burr may confer;
he shall return immediately with further interesting details;
this is essential to concert and harmony of movement. Send a
list of all persons known to Wilkinson west of the mountains
who could be useful, with a note deliniating their characters.
By your messenger, send me four or five commissions of your
officers, which you can borrow under any pretence you please;
they shall be returned faithfully. Already are orders given to the
contractor to forward six months' provisions to points Wilkinson may name; this shall not be used until the last moment, and
then under proper injunctions. Our object, my dear friend, is

*See Appendix D, Volume Three, Beveridge's "Life of John
Marshall."

brought to a point so long desired. Burr guarantees the result with his life and honor, with the lives and honor and the fortunes of hundreds, the best blood of our country. Burr's plan of operation is to move down rapidly from the Falls, on the fifteenth of November, with the first five hundred or a thousand men, in light boats now constructing for that purpose; to be at Natchez between the fifth and fifteenth of December, there to meet you; there to determine whether it will be expedient in the first instance to seize on or pass by Baton Rouge. On receipt of this send Burr an answer. Draw on Burr for all expenses, etc. The people of the country to which we are going are prepared to receive us; their agents, now with Burr, say that if we will protect their religion, and will not subject them to a foreign Power, that in three weeks all will be settled. The gods invite us to glory and fortune; it remains to be seen whether we deserve the boon. The bearer of this goes express to you. He is a man of inviolable honor and perfect discretion, formed to execute rather than project, capable of relating facts with fidelity, and incapable of relating them otherwise; he is thoroughly informed of the plans and intentions of Burr, and will disclose to you as far as you require, and no further. He has imbibed a reverence for your character, and may be embarrassed in your presence; put him at ease, and he will satisfy you.''

E

Names of Grand Jurors in Burr Trial

Names of Grand Jurors of Burr Trial, Burr Trials 45-46: John Randolph, Jr., Joseph Eggleston, Joseph C. Cabell, Littleton W. Tazewell, Robert Taylor, James Pleasants, John Brockenbrough, William Daniel, James M. Garnett, John Mercer, Edward Pegram, Munford Beverly, John Ambler, Thomas Harrison, Alexander Shepherd, and James Barbour.